DORSET FOLK TALES
for
CHILDREN

Tim Laycock

Illustrated by Zoe Barnish

Thanks to Zoe for her beautiful illustrations, and to Rosie, Bessie, Barley and Angela for listening to the stories and making many helpful suggestions.

First published 2019

The History Press
97 St George's Place
Cheltenham
GL50 3QB
www.thehistorypress.co.uk

© Tim Laycock, 2019
Illustrations © Zoe Barnish, 2019

The right of Tim Laycock to be identified as the Author
of this work has been asserted in accordance with the
Copyright, Designs and Patents Act 1988.

All rights reserved. No part of this book may be reprinted
or reproduced or utilised in any form or by any electronic,
mechanical or other means, now known or hereafter invented,
including photocopying and recording, or in any information
storage or retrieval system, without the permission in writing
from the Publishers.

British Library Cataloguing in Publication Data.
A catalogue record for this book is available from the British Library.

ISBN 978 0 7509 8776 9

Typesetting and origination by The History Press
Printed and bound in Great Britain by TJ Books, Padstow, Cornwall

DORSET FOLK TALES
for
CHILDREN

Contents

	About the Author	7
	Introduction	9
1	The Old Man of the Sea	11
2	Sidney Northover's Boots	27
3	The Wonderful Crocodile	39
4	Bincombe Bumps	51
5	Giant Grumble	67
6	The Drowners	81
7	Where's the Hare?	87
8	Jack and the Boat	93
9	The Map	109
10	Jack with a Lantern	119

11	The Beggar's Wedding	137
12	Granny Parsons and the Dorset Dumplings	151
13	The Merman	165
14	The Christmas Bull	177

About the Author

Tim Laycock grew up in North Dorset and loves singing the songs and telling the stories of the area. He works as a folk singer, musician and actor, and is fascinated by the history and culture of Dorset.

Introduction

Dorset is full of stories. Maybe it's something to do with the spectacular countryside and the Jurassic coast, or perhaps it's the wealth of ancient monuments and hill forts that surround us. Everywhere there are stories of strange happenings, heroic deeds, comedies and tragedies that put us in touch with the people that lived here in the past.

If you like these tales, why not come on down to Dorset and visit a few of the places where these stories come from? You could have a picnic on the beach at Burton Bradstock and see if you can spot the hotel that Alice longs for in 'The Old Man of the Sea'. You could climb up on to Poundbury Camp in Dorchester and look down on the water meadows of the River Frome, where the dragon disappeared. Go for a walk along the Ridgeway and listen to the music at Bincombe Bumps. Stroll around Dewlish, where Sidney Northover found the mammoth, or have tea in the park at Littlebredy, where Reuben Hansford went to school. I hope you enjoy these stories as much as I enjoy finding them and telling them!

Tim Laycock, 2019

1

The Old Man of the Sea

A LONG TIME AGO, when flax was grown in the fields around Burton Bradstock, there was an old fisherman called George Hansford. He lived with his wife Alice in a tiny cottage just behind the Hive beach, not far from the sea. A tumbledown kind of an old place it was, too, with one chimney, two little rooms downstairs, and a bedroom and a box room upstairs. The front room was filled with musical instruments – banjos, mandolins, squeezeboxes and mouth-organs; and whenever George made a bit of extra money from the fishing (which wasn't often), he'd buy another himself another instrument. There was no bathroom indoors, just an old privy in a little shed at the end of the garden! The garden looked like a shipyard: bits and pieces of masts, sails, fishing nets, fish boxes, anchors – all the things you need to catch fish in the sea.

Now, George had been at sea for forty years and what he didn't know about fishing wasn't worth knowing. But fishing is a hard way of making a living and there was never much money to spare, so when people began to move into the village and build nice bungalows along the road to the beach, with big picture windows and indoor bathrooms, Alice began to grumble.

'George, you need to work harder. You should catch more fish, and then we can have a proper, warm bathroom and an indoor loo. I'm fed up with that privy, especially in the winter.'

The old fisherman just grunted. He carried on baiting his crab pots. He loaded up his tackle and walked down to his boat with his wife's words ringing in his ears. He rowed out to sea, set the sail and sniffed the air. It always cheered him up, heading out to sea with the spray flying around his face, and the prospect of a few hours of peace and quiet bobbing around on the ocean.

He dropped his crab pots, cast his net and sat down to wait. After a while, he saw the net floats bobbing, and began to haul in, hoping for a decent catch. As the net came over the side of the boat, he saw an unfamiliar shape tangled up amongst the seaweed and the fish. The creature thrashed around in the mesh of the net and George stared, completely astonished. Was it a fish? It certainly had a long tail. Was it a seal? It certainly had sad brown eyes and whiskers. Was it even a very strange child? It was too old to be a baby, all wrinkled and wild looking.

The fisherman scratched his head. 'Well, I'm blowed! Whatever are you, and what do I do with you, eh?'

The sea creature wriggled round and sat on the side of the boat, and George could see that it had a long beard entwined with seaweed, and most of its body was covered in shimmering blue, silver and green scales. But it had arms just like a human and it stared at the fisherman, then buried its head in its hands and burst into tears. The sobs were pitiful to hear and George felt very sorry for the fish-man.

'Now then mate,' he said, 'don't take on like that. I won't hurt you. There's plenty of other fish in my net. I don't need to eat you too.'

'Oh thank you, thank you!' said the fish-man. 'I am the Old Man of the Sea. And for your kindness, I can grant you one wish. What shall it be? Anything at all, just ask!'

The fisherman thought about a new boat, or a new banjo. But then he remembered what his wife had said about the bathroom, so he said, 'It's not for me really, it's for Alice, my wife. She says our house is very cold in winter and we've only got an outside privy. Could we have a cosy indoor bathroom do you think?'

The Old Man of the Sea smiled. 'Of course, consider it done,' he said. And with that, he did a backflip off the side of the boat, waved his tail and disappeared into the sea.

George finished hauling in his nets and set sail for home. As he approached the beach, he looked through his telescope and saw his wife waiting for him on the seashore, and as he got closer he could see that she was dancing and singing.

'George!' she shouted. 'George, come and look! Come and see what's happened. It's wonderful! I can't believe it!'

The fisherman hauled his boat up on the shingle and followed his wife back to the cottage. There, sure enough, was a sparkling, shiny new bathroom: washbasin, bath, and toilet. The taps gleamed like silver and the tiles glinted in the light.

'How did it happen?' she said. 'Where did you get the money?'

Then the fisherman told his wife about the creature in the net and the wish, and that night they sat down to a good meal of fresh fish, happy as could be.

However, the next morning, Alice said, 'George, I've been thinking …' This was a bad sign; it usually meant that she would ask him to do something!

'Well…' Alice said, 'This story about the Old Man of the Sea … is it true?'

'Of course it is, my dear,' said George.

'Well prove it! I've been thinking that you were a bit daft, just to ask for an indoor bathroom. You could have asked for a nice new bungalow with a picture window, like the others up the road. I think you should go and catch that fish-man again, and this time ask him for nice new bungalow.'

George stared at her. 'You must be crazy,' he said. 'The chances of me catching him again must be one in ten thousand. He'll have swum off somewhere else, for certain.'

'Go and try,' she said.

So the fisherman loaded his nets and crab pots, and set off back to sea. He took his banjo with him and dropped anchor next to some rocks, where he always knew he would catch fish. Then he picked up his banjo and began to sing:

Man of the sea,
Come listen to me;
For Alice, my wife,

The joy of my life,
Has sent me to beg a boon of thee.

At first, nothing happened, but then the sea began to bubble and out jumped the Old Man of the Sea, and perched on the side of the boat.

'Ahoy there, shipmate!' he said. 'How do you like the bathroom?'

'Yes, it's very nice,' replied the fisherman. 'But Alice, well, she's not content with that! She wants a bungalow like the ones further up the road …'

'D'you mean the ones with the picture windows?' asked the Old Man of the Sea.

'Yes, that's it, if you don't mind?'

The Old Man of the Sea looked thoughtful. 'Well, that's a second wish, but I suppose I can allow it. Consider it done,' he said. And with that he did a double backflip off the side of the boat, waved his tail and disappeared into the sea.

The fisherman finished hauling in his nets and set sail for home. As he approached the beach, he looked through his telescope and saw his wife waiting for him on the seashore, and as he got closer he could see that she was dancing and singing.

'George!' she shouted. 'George, come and look! Come and see what's happened. It's wonderful! I can't believe it.'

The fisherman hauled his boat up onto the shingle and followed his wife back – but where was his house? It had completely disappeared. And there, sure enough, in its place was a beautiful new bungalow.

'It's what I've always wanted!' she said. 'Come inside, my dear, and mind you wipe your feet!'

Then George told his wife about the song and the banjo, and how the Old Man of the Sea sat on the boat, and the second wish; and that night they sat down to a good meal of fresh fish, happy as could be.

All went well for a week or so, and then one morning the fisherman noticed his wife looking out from her great front window. She was gazing towards the sea.

'What are you looking at?' he asked.

'I've been thinking George … you could have asked for a nice hotel, like the one on the headland there. Then you could give up the fishing and be head waiter. There are so many tourists round here these days, we'd make a fortune! I could be the manager. Go and catch that fish-man again, and this time ask him for a hotel!'

George stared at her. 'You must be crazy,' he said. 'The chances of catching the fish-man again must be one in a million. He'll have swum off somewhere else, for certain!'

'Go and try,' she said.

So the fisherman loaded his nets and crab pots and set off back to sea. He took his mandolin with him and dropped his anchor over a sandbank, where he always knew he would catch fish. Then he picked up his mandolin and began to sing:

Man of the sea,
Come listen to me;
For Alice, my wife,
The joy of my life,
Has sent me to beg a boon of thee.

At first, nothing happened, but then the sea began to bubble and out jumped the fish-man, and perched on the side of the boat.

'Good morning, matey,' he said. 'How do you like the bungalow?'

The fisherman groaned. 'As far as I'm concerned, it's perfect.'

'So why have you come back?'

'It's not for me,' he said. 'It's Alice – she wants a hotel, just like the one on the headland. Can you help us?'

The fish-man rubbed his chin and thought hard. 'Well, I suppose three wishes might be allowed – but only three, mind. Consider it done.' And with that he did a triple backflip off the side of the boat, waved his tail and disappeared into the sea.

The fisherman finished hauling in his nets and set sail for home. As he approached the beach, he looked through his telescope and saw his wife waiting for him on the top of the cliff above the beach, dancing and singing. Behind her, its great glass windows reflecting the setting sun, was a brand new hotel with a great flashing sign, surrounded with a beautiful garden, a tennis court and a swimming pool.

'George!' she shouted. 'George, come and look! Come and see what's happened. It's wonderful! I can't believe it!'

The fisherman hauled his boat up onto the shingle, and made his way up to the hotel. And for a month or so, the business thrived, and Alice was very happy.

But one morning, as they were sat having coffee in the sun room overlooking Lyme Bay, she said, 'George, I've been thinking …'

His heart sank; he knew what was coming!

'I think you were a bit modest, just asking for a hotel. Go back and ask him for a castle. Not a ruined one like Corfe Castle. A nice one, with huge rooms and paintings and curtains, like Windsor Castle. I'll be Queen, and you can be King. Go and ask him for a castle!'

George stared at her. 'You must be crazy,' he said. 'The chances of catching him again must be one in a hundred million. He'll have swum off somewhere else, for certain.'

'Go and try,' she said.

'But the Old Man said, "No more wishes."'

'Go and try!'

So, very reluctantly, the fisherman loaded his nets and crab pots and set off back to sea. He took his squeezebox with him and dropped his anchor over a shipwreck, where he always knew he would catch fish. Then he picked up his squeezebox and began to sing:

> Man of the sea,
> Come listen to me;
> For Alice, my wife,
> The joy of my life,
> Has sent me to beg a boon of thee.

At first, nothing happened, but then the sea began to bubble and out jumped the Man of the Sea, and perched on the side of the boat.

'Good morning, matey,' he said. 'How do you like the hotel?'

'Very good,' said the fisherman. 'But you see, it's Alice – this time she wants a castle.'

'Oh, does she now?' said the fish-man. 'Oh, does she now? Well, that's one wish too many!'

And with that he did a quadruple backflip, waved his tail and dived into the sea.

The fisherman sat quietly for a few minutes, staring at the spot where the fish-man had disappeared. Then he hauled in his nets and set sail for home. As he approached the beach, there was no one waiting for him on the seashore. The hotel on the headland had vanished. He walked up the road and the bungalow with picture windows had vanished. All that was left was his little cottage on the seashore, and up at the end of the garden was a little wooden privy – even the new indoor bathroom had gone!

Alice was sobbing on the doorstep.

'Never you mind, my love,' said George kindly. 'At least we've got some fresh fish for tea.'

'Oh, George, it's all my fault. I was too greedy, and now everything's gone!'

'Not everything, my dear. Come on inside. We've still got the fish – it's mackerel, your favourite, and there's nothing in the world better than a plate of fresh Burton mackerel!'

Reverend Henry Moule was the vicar in Fordington, Dorchester. He had lots of children, and he heard this song being sung by their nursemaid. The tale is found in many cultures around the world.

2

Sidney Northover's Boots

HAVE YOU EVER put your foot into your welly and felt something warm and wriggly squirming about inside? I bet if you did, you'd pull your foot out pretty quick and shake out your boot. You might even scream! Or you might just push your foot in anyway, and hobble around until someone noticed and told you to take your boot off – and out would run a confused spider, or even a mouse, and scurry off under the sofa!

In the days before rubber wellies, when everyone wore leather boots or wooden-soled clogs, Sidney Northover was working in the fields with his father and a great gang of men and women. As it was the school holidays, the children were helping. They were all busy bringing in the harvest. The weather had been kind all week, and the foreman was very pleased. They'd finished most of the fields, and the wheat and barley stacks behind Manor Farm in Dewlish were rising above the roofs of the farmyard buildings. Everyone was in a good mood and the wheat and barley promised plenty of winter work. Even old Phil Humphries had a song on his lips, and all was well in the world.

> Oats and beans and barley grows.
> As you and I and everyone knows.
> Oats and beans and barley grows
> As you and I and everyone know,
> Waiting for your partner!
>
> First the farmer sows his seed,
> Then he stands and takes his ease.
> Takes his ease and claps his hands
> And turns around to view the land,
> Waiting for your partner!

But all wasn't well with Sidney Northover – his boots were too tight. The cobbler in Milborne St Andrew had promised his mother that the leather was supple and it would certainly stretch as Sid's feet grew. Well, if that was going to happen, it hadn't happened yet! The boots made him hobble around and the other children would laugh at him. But his mother couldn't afford more boots, so Sid had to put up with it.

At midday, the harvesters sat under the waggon in the shade to eat their bread and cheese and to drink their cold tea. Sid crept away on his own to the great hazel hedge that ran around the top end of the field. He sat down, eased off his pinching boots, and took out his lunch.

His back was weary from bending to pick up the wheat ears, and he curled up for a short nap. As he slept, he had a dream. He was far away from Dewlish, on board a great sailing ship, standing in the crow's nest as the vessel neared land.

Sid looked through his telescope. 'Land Ho!' he shouted.

'Where away?' cried the mate below.

'On the starboard bow sir, and it's coming up fast!' A boat was launched, with Sid in command. They landed on a deserted beach. Tropical palms came right down to the waterline, and brightly coloured birds flew above their heads.

'Follow me everyone, keep close together and look out!'

The intrepid boy led the landing party into the trees. Soon they were surrounded by dense vegetation. Everywhere they could smell the hot sweet scents of the jungle. They were startled by strange cries and calls. Suspicious rustles in the undergrowth made them all very nervous.

'Follow me, keep close together and look out!' warned Sid.

Then, all of a sudden, they heard a tremendous trumpeting and the sound of breaking branches and crashing trees. Right in front of them, terrible and terrifying, stood a great bull elephant, its tusks festooned in branches. It was glaring straight at them! The rest of the landing party turned tail and ran, but Sid stood his ground. He pulled off one of his boots, ready to throw it at the elephant. But just as the elephant was about to charge, the most peculiar thing happened. A small mouse ran across the path, right in front of the great animal's foot. The elephant took one look, waved its trunk in alarm, turned tail and –

'Wake up, Sid! Get your boots on! Time to start work again!'

'Eh? What?' Sid looked up to see his father grinning at him.

'Wake up, sleepyhead! You've been daydreaming! Get cracking, my son. We're not finished yet, there's two more fields to do before sunset.'

Sid tried to pull on his boots. There was something wriggling in his left boot. Something warm and squiggly – a mouse! He shook the mouse out and it ran a short way, then turned and looked, as if to say, 'Thank you kindly.'

'Not at all,' said Sid politely. 'I'm sure that boot is more comfortable for you than it is for me!'

The mouse turned and ran to the bank, then stopped and looked again. And then she scurried back a little further, stopped and looked.

'Are you trying to show me something?' asked Sid.

The mouse just kept on looking at him. Sid crept forward. The mouse ran back a little way and then stopped and looked again. Sid followed her, and he saw a patch of yellow sand amongst the leaves and grasses in the hedge. He went closer to examine it. He knew that the farmer had sent to Dorchester for several cartloads of sand only last week and had complained at the price of it. Yet here was some sand in the hillside just above Long Meadow – maybe quite a lot! Sid picked up a handful and tied it up in his handkerchief.

'Sidney Northover, get yourself down here at once!' It was Farmer Tuck, and he sounded very angry. Sid forced on his boots and hobbled painfully down the hill.

'What the blazes do you think you're up to?' demanded the farmer. 'I don't pay you to lie around and be idle. Get on with your work!'

'I only took my boots off for a minute 'cos they pinch,' said Sid, 'and I had a dream about a mouse and an elephant and then I found this –' and he held out his handkerchief.

The farmworkers all looked anxious. No one had ever dared to answer back to the farmer!

'How dare you talk back to me!' roared the farmer. 'I don't want to hear your excuses!' Then he looked at Sid's handkerchief, and his expression changed. He took it, and he poured the sand into his hand.

'Where did you find this?' he asked.

'Just the other side of the hazel hedge up there.' Sid pointed to the spot.

'Well, hmmm! Well – you get back to work, and we'll say no more about it. A mouse and an elephant, eh?' The farmer chuckled, and the farmworkers all stared in amazement – he hardly ever laughed!

The harvest continued. At last everything was safely gathered in, and the weather changed. Autumn began, and the children went back to school. One day, as Sid was sitting at the kitchen table having his tea, there was a knock on the door. His mother answered and she stayed talking with someone for quite a long time. Then she called her son.

'Here's Mr Tuck come to see you Sidney,' she said, and she sounded pleased.

'Well, my lad, I've come to say thank you! I thought I knew my own land, but you know it better! You and that mouse of yours found sand, lots of it. I'd never have thought of looking for it above Long Meadow! I'm very grateful to you and I'd like you to have these.' He handed Sid a brown paper package.

'Go on Sidney, open it,' said his mother. Inside was the best pair of boots Sid had ever seen. He sat down and tried them on straight away. They fitted perfectly.

'Thank you ever so much!' he said. 'They're the most comfortable boots I've ever had!'

But that wasn't quite the end of the story. The workmen kept on digging sand for weeks.

Just before Bonfire Night, the schoolmistress told her students there would be no work that afternoon; they were all going on a nature walk.

'It's all to do with Sidney Northover's boots,' she said mysteriously.

They walked through the village and up the hill until they came to the sandpit. In the middle were a group of grown-ups staring at something, and working in a big hole in the sand. The children gathered round to look.

'Children, this is Captain Acland. He's from the museum in Dorchester. He's got something very exciting to show us!'

The man stood up. In the sand they could see a pile of enormous bones. At one end was a great skull, with tusks attached.

'That's my elephant!' shouted Sid.

Captain Acland laughed. 'You must be the famous Sidney Northover! I've heard all about you. Well, Sidney, it's not quite an elephant – it's a lot older. This is the skeleton of a mammoth. It lived in your village nearly ten thousand years ago.'

The children were amazed. Some of them patted Sid on the back.

'So when I had a dream about an elephant, I was nearly right?'

'Very nearly,' replied the Captain. 'I think that all this sand was once a river bed, and this mammoth must have died here all those years ago. It's a wonderful find – and all thanks to your pinching boots.'

'Three cheers for Sidney Northover's boots!' shouted Mary Spencer.

'Hip, hip, hip, hooray!'
'Hip, hip, hip, hooray!'
'Hip, hip, hip, HOORAY!'

3

The Wonderful Crocodile

Come listen people unto me, to tell you the truth I'm bound;
What happened to me when I went to sea, and the wonders that I found ...

My name is Jane Hann. My mother died when I was ten years old, and I was looked after by my father. He was the captain of a sailing ship and whenever he went on a voyage, I went with him. The ship was called *The Cygnet*, and when my adventures began, she was bound for Portugal with a cargo of salted codfish. In the middle of the Atlantic Ocean, we were hit by a terrible storm. We were driven south with such fury and force that we thought our last hour had come. After three days and nights, *The Cygnet* was swamped by a tremendous wave. It broke the ship's back and flung us all into the sea – all except my father. The last I ever saw of him was a solitary figure, standing bravely at the ship's wheel as *The Cygnet* slipped beneath the waves.

I tried my best to swim, although I knew it was hopeless. My heavy clothes would drag me down and I would surely drown. But then a length of broken mast drifted by, trailing snapped ropes. I was able to cling on and tie myself to the timber. Fortunately, the water was not cold. Exhausted by storm and shipwreck, I drifted on in a kind of confused dream.

When I awoke, the storm had passed. The sea was calm, and the sun shone. I looked around, and I saw a low-lying island in front of me. The waves were gently propelling me towards land, and soon I was able to feel the seabed beneath my feet. I dragged myself up the beach. I called out loud, but no one answered. There was no sign of any other living person around. I took off my wet clothes and laid them out to dry.

Where was I? What would happen to me? What could I eat? Who would come to help me?

'Come along, Jane,' I said to myself. 'Pull yourself together! This won't do! Find food and shelter first and worry about everything else later.' Luckily, I had my trusty penknife in my jacket pocket.

I made my way inland, and came across a ruined house. It had an overgrown garden full of tropical fruits. Behind the house was a deep well. I lowered the bucket and drew up fresh, cool water. I feasted on fruit, and spent the night alone in the house, with the door barricaded and a heap of grass and leaves for my bed.

In the morning I set off to explore. I followed the coastline and it took me more than a week to walk around my island. In all this time I never saw another human being, or any creature larger than a deer. On the eighth day of my walk I was surprised by a great movement in the land ahead. The hill in front of me began to move and shake! I was very afraid that it might be an earthquake; but then I was astonished to see a monstrous head rear up, open its mighty jaws and snap them shut again.

This was no earthquake – I was standing on the back of an enormous crocodile, many miles long!

Of course, I had read of crocodiles, and seen pictures in my encyclopaedia, but I never expected to meet such a giant as this! I quickly ran to a very tall tree. I climbed up as high as I could. By my reckoning, the crocodile was fifty miles long. I could see two great horns reaching out from the crocodile's head and disappearing in the direction of the moon. As I watched, a small boy appeared from the forest, ran nimbly up the crocodile's side and along his back, and began to climb up one of the horns. The crocodile, meanwhile, slumbered peacefully, occasionally snorting and stirring. The boy disappeared into the clouds and was gone.

I decided to wait until he came down. I found plenty of branches and pieces of wood. With my trusty penknife I cut down creepers, and in a few days I had made a treehouse where I could safely live and watch the enormous crocodile.

It was six months before the boy reappeared, clutching a large cheese. When I asked him what he'd seen, and where he had found his cheese, he took one look at me and ran off into the woods. A piece of the cheese broke off as he ran away and I decided to keep it. During the day, it was a dull green colour, but at night it glowed brightly in the dark. I tried it for taste, and decided it was something between a Cheddar and a Wensleydale, with the texture of a Stilton.

All of a sudden, the wind began to blow from the south. Soon my treehouse was bending and listing in the storm, and I was holding on for dear life. But it was no use; I was blown right out of the tree towards the sleeping crocodile. He opened his eye, and a devilish glint appeared. His great jaws opened swiftly, and before I had the chance to escape, they closed with a snap! I was caught: trapped in the mouth of the biggest crocodile in the world. I quickly slid down the crocodile's throat, to get away from his terrible teeth.

This tickled the crocodile's tongue, and he coughed and spluttered, which tumbled me further down inside the creature's gullet.

The smell was appalling. I couldn't see anything. Then, in the murky darkness, I heard a bell ringing, and beautiful singing echoing through the crocodile's cavernous throat. Using my glowing cheese as a lantern, I made my way towards the music. There, much to my surprise, was a clergyman in cassock and surplice, ringing a church bell. He was surrounded by choirboys and choirgirls, singing a Christmas carol. When the song finished, I thanked them, and offered them all a taste of my cheese. Then I bid them all farewell and I continued my journey into the depths of the crocodile.

After a day or so, I began to feel a deep pulsing and beating. When I came around the corner, I saw a gigantic red heart, slowly expanding and contracting as it pumped the lifeblood of the reptile through great white pipes. With the greatest difficulty, I squeezed past and made my way further into the uncharted interior of the monster.

It was now becoming more difficult to breathe, and the light of my cheese was growing dim. I was afraid that I was so far from the open air that I would die for lack of breath. Suddenly, a great gale of fresh air blew in my face, followed at regular intervals by more. My cheese flared up and I was amazed to see two great bellows of enormous size, expanding and contracting with a slow, deep regularity. These, I decided, must be the creature's lungs. As one lung went in, so the other went out, as regular as clockwork; and I marvelled at the precision of nature and the wonderful way in which this gigantic creature was constructed.

I continued my journey through the subterranean corridors and passageways of the great beast. I found very little to eat, although there was plenty of water everywhere. At last I came to a great, wide, open space. A flock of birds flew overhead and all around were green fields and woods. A small stream babbled its way between shady trees, and nearby stood an orchard of apple, pear and cherry trees, all laden with fruit. I lay under the oldest apple tree and enjoyed the fruits. These apples were the most delicious that I have ever tasted. Then I saw a small shed. On a table were several Cheddar cheeses and a row of ginger beer bottles. Taking a plate and a tankard, I cut myself a piece of cheese and drew a pint of beer.

'These,' I said to myself, 'are better rations than a sailor gets aboard *The Cygnet*!'

The country I had found inside the crocodile had everything that anyone could possibly want. I lived there very happily for nearly ten years.

At last, however, I became aware that all was not well with my crocodile. His breathing became laboured, and slowed, and then finally one morning everything was silent and still. I ran back to the creature's lungs. There was no movement. I ran back to his heart. It had stopped beating. I quickly realised my danger: without a supply of fresh air, my own days were numbered, and the fruit trees in the orchard were already showing signs of distress. I had to escape as quickly as possible.

I took my trusty penknife and carved a spade. I rolled up my sleeves and began to dig. It took me six months to dig my way through the crocodile, for his skin was two miles thick. My supply of cheese and ginger beer was all gone when at last I began to see daylight, and on the 1st of April 1810 I finally dug my way out of the crocodile. I ate my last apple and popped the core in my pocket. Then I climbed down his side and made my way back to the shore of the island.

As I walked along the beach, dazzled by the brightness of the sunlight, I saw a ship on the horizon. Quickly I lit a great bonfire. At last a boat came ashore, and I was taken on board HMS *Osprey* and carried back to England. I arrived safe and sound in Portsmouth fifteen years and three months after leaving St Johns, Newfoundland, on board *The Cygnet*.

Of course, the captain and crew of HMS *Osprey* were very intrigued by my story, but politely expressed their doubts whether any young person could have experienced such an extraordinary adventure. However, I was able to prove the truth of it by showing them my trusty penknife and the apple core from the last apple taken from the tree inside the crocodile's stomach. Now, of course, that apple core has perished, and so you must trust the truth of this story to the word of the storyteller.

Jane Hann, Dorsetshire, 1812.

This story exists in Dorset as a folksong called the 'Wonderful Crocodile', which was sung in Buckland Newton.

4

Bincombe Bumps

OUR SCHOOLMASTER WAS called Mr Hawkins, but when he wasn't listening we all called him Turkey, because he went bright red from the neck upwards whenever he was cross or flustered. Turkey told us, last thing one September afternoon, that the following day we must all write an essay on 'adventures after school'. That made us scratch our heads, for as far as we knew, there wouldn't be any. Our village was a tiny, quiet sort of place, tucked away below Bincombe Hill, where nothing much happened – leastways, nothing we could tell him about!

After school and a bit of tea, we all met up as usual.

'What shall we play tonight?'

'HARE AND HOUNDS!'

That was the big favourite, a kind of hide and seek that took us all through the village and up the lane onto the Ridgeway. Mary set off and we hid our eyes and counted to 100, then began to sing out:

'HOLLER FOLLER! HOLLER FOLLER!'

From way up the lane, out of the gathering gloom, came the reply: 'FOLLER!'

Off we went, scrambling all over the hill trying to catch her. We'd been playing for an hour or so, when the game led us past Widow Diment's orchard. We all leaned over the wall. The trees were heavy with apples, just waiting to be picked. Do we dare? What about Lazy Lawrence?

Widow Diment's orchard produced wonderful apples every autumn. They were the most delicious apples that anyone had ever tasted, and that's saying something. When she took them to Dorchester market to sell, she made enough money to keep her comfortable for the rest of the year.

She was a very old-fashioned lady, and she kept up the old ways. Every night she would put out a bowl of cream and another of spring water, for she knew that there were those who guarded orchards and she wanted to do right by them.

Some folk thought she put the cream out for the birds or the hedgehogs, but we children all knew it was for Lazy Lawrence, a dainty little colt-pixie that lived in these parts. Strange name for such a lively creature really; he could run like the wind and he could jump hedges as if they were only inches high. Very few people had ever seen him, but plenty of boys and girls had felt the nip of his teeth when they crept into orchards at night to scrump a few apples. You must never make the slightest sound if you wanted to scrump, because Lazy Lawrence would hear you and come at a gallop. And whatever you did, you must never look into his eyes. Blazing green, they were, and if once he caught you in his gaze, you'd be transfixed to the spot until it pleased him to let you go. That's why we all knew a rhyme that went:

Lazy Lawrence, let me go,
Don't make me wait an hour or so.

Years ago, there was an old conjuror who lived on Purbeck. Black-hearted old fella he was, and he'd heard about the old widow's apples. One night he decided to help himself, but being in the conjuring trade he knew all about Lazy Lawrence, and was wary of those green eyes and sharp teeth. So he climbed into a great apple hamper and conjured up a spell that sent the hamper tumbling into the middle of the orchard. Then he conjured up another spell that sent all the widow's apples raining down onto the ground in a great circle, and some of them flew right into the hamper itself. One particularly large one struck the old conjuror such a blow on his head that he yelled out – and that was his big mistake. Lazy Lawrence heard him and jumped over the hedge and into the orchard in an instant. He kicked the hamper all over the place, conjuror and all! When he tried to climb out, Lazy Lawrence caught him with those green eyes and made him stand still as a statue.

Well, next morning – what a sight! There was the conjuror, unable to move, with all the apples in a great circle around him and the hamper broken all to pieces. And around the apples was a circle of hoofprints, so people knew that Lazy Lawrence had helped the widow. They could have called him all sorts of names, or slung mud at him, but they didn't because they knew that would break the spell, and the conjuror would have been free. Instead, they made him wait there until the dew was dried by the sun and the footprints disappeared; and then the conjuror was able to make his way, all kicked and bruised, off down the road towards Wareham. The folk all set to and brought baskets and pails for the widow's apples, took them to the market, and sold them for a very good price. Well, as they say:

'An apple a day keeps the doctor away – and also the conjuror!'

Susan went over that orchard wall quiet as a mouse, picked a few apples and passed them to us. We were just pulling her back over the wall when suddenly Widow Diment appeared on her bicycle, waving her umbrella and shouting:

'Stop thief! STOP! STOP! STOP!'

Off we ran down the lane, with the widow in hot pursuit. We dodged behind the bus shelter and she went sailing past, still calling out at the top of her voice – I reckon she was enjoying herself!

Soon we were ready for more fun. There were two old chaps called Gunner and Charlie who lived next door to each other up in Church Lane, but they didn't get on, always arguing about one thing or another. One of us crept up with a piece of string and tied their door handles together, knocked on both doors and ran off. Well, there was an almighty row, and then they looked down the lane and saw us, so we all ran away. But Gunner and Charlie came after us and nearly knocked the widow off her bicycle, so she joined in the chase, all of them shouting out, 'STOP! STOP! STOP!'

We headed up towards the Ridgeway and began to sing:

Run, run, as fast as you can,
You can't catch us, we're Billy Grey's gang!

At the top of the lane was the village hall. It was Women's Institute night. We stopped to peer in through the window, and there were all the village ladies sitting on the hard wooden chairs, listening carefully to a lady in a great hat.

'Let's put a bag over the chimney,' said Billy. 'Just like we did a fortnight ago.' But the others said no, the ladies were wise to that, and then Mary piped up:

'What about Nazareth?'

Nazareth was the farmer's donkey, kept in the field by the wood. With the aid of a couple of Widow Diment's apples, we got him out and down to the hall, where we opened the door, smacked the donkey's bum and in he went, hee-hawing away. Oh, my goodness, glorious confusion! We legged it again, and it didn't take those women long to get the donkey out and chase after us, so now there was Nazareth the donkey and the WI ladies and Gunner and Charlie, and the Widow Diment on her bicycle, all puffing and panting and crying out 'STOP! STOP! STOP!' and again we sung out:

Run, run, as fast as you can,
You can't catch us, we're Billy Grey's gang!

We ran right to the top of the Ridgeway until we could see the sea.

Suddenly we stopped, arrested in our tracks by a blue light. Was it a police car? But no, the blue light was not on the road, it was out at sea, and there's people down on the beach landing something – and then, in the darkness, we heard the tramping of heavy feet and a low hum of voices:

> In South Australia I was born,
> Heave away, Haul away,
> South Australia round Cape Horn,
> We're bound for South Australia.

We were pressed into the bushes beside the track, scarcely daring to breathe. The voices got closer. They came past us, so close we could see the whites of their eyes, the casks slung round their necks and the leader, a tall man in a wide-brimmed hat, anxiously looking around him all the time.

'Steady there lads ... Aye, aye Emmanuel ... Keep them tubs moving – quickly now!'

Suddenly we were grabbed by strong hands.

'What the devil are ye doing here?'

'Are they Revenue?'

'No, kids, Mr Charles. Spying on us!'

Then Billy suddenly turned. He managed to bite the hand of the chap that was holding him. The smuggler cursed and fell over the tubs he was carrying. In the confusion, the rest of us broke free and hared off back up the Ridgeway. We didn't stop until we reached the gorse bushes on the top. We crept along under the shelter of a hedge. Somewhere behind us in the dark was Emmanuel Charles and the smugglers, Nazareth the donkey, the WI ladies, Gunner and Charlie and the Widow Diment on her bicycle, all calling out faintly in the distance 'STOP! STOP! STOP!'

We were too frightened to sing, so we just looked at each other, grinned and whispered:

>Run, run, as fast as you can,
>You can't catch us, we're Billy Grey's gang!

We climbed onwards, until we came to some great mounds, black against the night sky.

'Where are we?' asked Mary.

'Bincombe Bumps, of course,' said Bill. 'We'll hide here, get our breath back.'

We huddled down in the darkness amongst the barrows. Strange eerie places they are at night, I can tell you. Some people reckon they're the graves of old warriors. Others say there's treasure in them, and we always look in the molehills and rabbit burrows in the hope of finding some, but we never have. As we lay in the grass, we began to hear a murmur, then a whisper. The whisper grew into the beginnings of a tune, and then real music, humming music. First of all it came from one barrow, then the second one joined it, and then all of them. We were properly spooked by that, so we legged it again, away from the singing bumps, and headed full pelt along the Ridgeway until we saw a big, stout chap on a horse right in front of us. And the strangest thing was that the horse was completely white – and so was the rider.

'Hello there!' he calls out. 'What are you children doing out so late, eh?'

'Playing games, sir. We've got lost – we've got to get home.'

'Then jump up on my horse, I'm going your way! Always happy to go to Weymouth!'

We all managed to climb on the back of the horse, the whole gang of us! Billy was hanging on to the rider, though his arms could scarcely reach around his waist. The rider dug his spurs in and away we went, top speed. All along the top of the Ridgeway we rode in the moonlight.

The sea was away on the left and the lights of Dorchester away in the distance on the right. The horse went full pelt, trot, canter, gallop, and the strangest thing of all was that her hooves made no sound at all on the moonlit turf.

When we looked back, we could just make out the Singing Bumps, and behind them the smugglers, and Nazareth the donkey, and the WI ladies, Gunner and Charlie, and the Widow Diment on her bicycle, all shaking their fists in our direction, but there was nothing they could do!

'Halt! Who goes there?'

We stopped. In front of us, standing tall and barring the way, stood a commanding figure in a cocked hat and greatcoat, with a telescope under his arm. Behind him, in the dark, we could make out hundreds of shadowy faces, all staring at us.

'We can't go any further my dears!' said our horseman. 'That's my son, the Grand Old Duke of York! He's marched ten thousand men up to the top of the hill and there's no way through! This is where we must part company. There's your way home. Goodnight!'

And with that, he turned the horse about and galloped off in the direction of Osmington, leaving us to pick our way down the hill and back to our various homes.

'Listen,' said Bill, before we parted. 'We don't say a word – all agreed?'

'Agreed.'

'And when we get to school tomorrow, this is what we'll write…'

We all went into a huddle and he whispered in our ears.

So the next day, at school, Turkey Hawkins set us all the essay and gave us half an hour to write it. At the end of the half hour, he called in the papers, and every single one of us had written:

Last night I had no adventures at all, because I had to stay in to do my homework.

Well, Turkey went bright red, but he knew when he was beaten; and he never did find out what happened on Bincombe Hill the night we played Holler Foller!

5

Giant Grumble

Giant Grumble

GIANT GRUMBLE WAS always hungry. Every morning he would come down to his breakfast and shout:

I am Giant Grumble,
You can hear my tummy rumble!

'Yes, I can,' said his mother. 'What would you like for breakfast, Giant Grumble?'

'I want porridge!' the youngster replied.

'Pardon?' said his mother.

'I want porridge!' said Giant Grumble, louder this time.

'I beg your pardon?' said his mother, but Giant Grumble just bellowed.

'I WANT PORRIDGE! PORRIDGE, PORRIDGE, PORRIDGE!'

'Well, if you're going to be as rude as that, you can't have any,' said his mother, and instead she handed him a large yellow key. 'Go upstairs, and open the yellow cupboard.'

Giant Grumble stomped up the stairs, and opened up the yellow cupboard. Inside was a large pair of yellow boots. They looked about the right size, so he sat down and pulled them on. Then he noticed that on one of the boots was a label that said:

One Mile Boots.

Giant Grumble didn't know what that meant, but he soon found out! When he stood up and took one step, he went one mile, which was a big step even by giant standards. When he'd taken two steps, he was two miles away. After twenty steps he was right in the middle of Dorset, and then he saw a village shop. Displayed in the windows were all sorts of delicious fruits and vegetables.

Giant Grumble looked and licked his lips and thought to himself, 'Mmmmmmm! Apples, oranges and pears! That's what I'll have for breakfast.'

So he banged on the door and the shopkeeper said, 'Good morning young sir. Can I help you?'

Giant Grumble shouted, 'I want apples, oranges and pears!'

The shopkeeper said, 'Pardon?'

Giant Grumble roared, 'I want apples, oranges and pears!'

'I beg your pardon?' said the shopkeeper.

Giant Grumble was furious. 'I WANT APPLES, ORANGES AND PEARS!'

The shopkeeper was not intimidated by this display of temper.

'Well, if you're going to be as rude as that, I won't serve you!' she said and she shut the door, and hung up a little sign that said 'Closed for Lunch'.

Giant Grumble had to go all the way home, put the yellow boots back in the cupboard, and that night he went to bed very hungry.

Next morning Giant Grumble came down for breakfast, and he was starving:

I am Giant Grumble,
You can hear my tummy rumble!

'Yes, I can,' said his mother. 'What would you like for breakfast, Giant Grumble?'

'I want porridge!' the youngster replied.

'Pardon?' said his mother.

'I want porridge!' said Giant Grumble.

'I beg your pardon?' said his mother, and Giant Grumble bellowed

'I WANT PORRIDGE!'

'Well, if you're going to be as rude as that, you can't have any,' said his mother, and instead she handed him a large red key.

'Go upstairs, Giant Grumble, and open the red cupboard.'

Giant Grumble stomped upstairs, grumbling to himself all the way. But Giant Grumble was just like you or me: he was curious and he wondered what was in the red cupboard.

He tried the red key in the lock. The red cupboard swung open, and inside was a fine pair of red boots. He tried them on, and they fitted perfectly. He stood up, and noticed a label on one of the boots. This time the label said:

Two Mile Boots.

With one step he went two miles, with ten steps he went twenty miles, and before long he'd walked right up the country into Scotland.

He looked around him, sniffed, and smelt the most delicious smell.

'Mmmmmmm! Vinegar! Fish and Chips! That's what I'll have for breakfast!'

So he went up to the shop and shouted in through the doorway.

'I want fish and chips!'

'Pardon?' said the owner.

'I want fish and chips!'

'I beg your pardon?'

'Don't you understand plain English?' said Giant Grumble rudely. 'I WANT FISH AND CHIPS!'

'Well, laddie, if ye're going tae be sae rude as that, ye can't have any!' replied the owner briskly.

He went inside, shut up the shop and hung up a little notice on the door which said

'Gone to Lunch'. So Giant Grumble had to go all the way back home, still hungry. He put the boots back in the cupboard and that night he could scarcely sleep at all. His belly rumbled so loudly that houses shook all over Dorset, and ships were driven onto Chesil Beach by the waves at sea.

Next morning, he came downstairs in a terrible temper.

I am Giant Grumble,
You can hear my tummy rumble!

'Yes, I can; it's kept most of Dorset awake all night!' said his mother. 'What would you like for breakfast, Giant Grumble?'

'I want porridge!'

'Pardon?' said his mother.

'I want porridge!' said Giant Grumble.

'I beg your pardon?' said his mother, but Giant Grumble just bellowed.

'I WANT PORRIDGE!'

'I want, doesn't get,' said his mother, and instead she handed him a large blue key. She told him to go upstairs and open the blue cupboard.

'Yellow cupboards, red cupboards and now blue cupboards. I don't want cupboards, I WANT PORRIDGE!'

'Giant Grumble, please do as you're told,' said his mother quietly, and there was something in her tone of voice that got through to the angry giant. He turned, went upstairs and opened the blue cupboard. Inside was a pair of blue boots. Not any old blue either, but a deep, rich blue that seemed to promise adventure, distant lands and tropical seas. He put them on, and they fitted perfectly. One of them had a label that read:

Five Mile Boots.

Now, the thing with Five Mile Boots is that not only can you walk five miles with every step, you can also walk on water. Giant

Grumble walked down to Weymouth in two steps. He walked across to France, down to Italy, then through Greece and Turkey, until at last he came to a hot country called Lebanon. He stared at the date palms, and then sniffed.

'Mmmmmmmmm!'

It was the most delicious smell he'd ever smelt, a mixture of cream and spices and new bread. It was coming from a little house. He looked in through the window and he saw a woman. She was making scones, placing them on a baking tray and putting them into an oven. At the same time, she was stirring a large bowl of thick clotted cream. Giant Grumble's eyes widened, and he licked his lips.

'I want some of those,' he said.

The lady said, 'Pardon?'

Giant Grumble said, 'I want some of those.'

The lady said, 'I beg your pardon?'

Giant Grumble bellowed, 'Are you stupid? Don't you understand me? I WANT SOME OF THOSE!'

'Manners never cost anyone a penny,' she replied, and closed the shutters.

Giant Grumble was really fed up. He was hot, and he was bothered. Worst of all, he was REALLY hungry! He went away in a huff and sat in the shade under a great palm tree.

He felt very sorry for himself. He was so hungry he could hardly speak, he'd travelled hundreds of miles and the blue boots were beginning to pinch. Worst of all, he'd had the misfortune to end up in a country where grown-ups spoke in riddles. He eased the boots off.

Gradually the scented air and the delicious smells wafting from the house began to calm him down. He thought hard about everything that had happened over the last three days, and at last he had an idea. He went over to the house and tapped gently on the shutters. The lady opened the window and looked at him.

'Yes?'

'I want some of those, please,' said Giant Grumble hopefully.

A smile broke over the lady's face. 'Why, of course you can, Giant Grumble!' she said. 'Sit down over there, and I'll bring them out when they are ready.'

First of all, she brought out a large, brightly coloured tablecloth and tied it round his neck for a bib. Next, she bought out a silver tray. It was piled high with fresh scones, clotted cream, jam, honey and a pot of tea.

Giant Grumble couldn't decide whether to put the cream on the scones first, or the jam; so in the end he tried them both ways, and each way was equally delicious.

He didn't stop eating until the food was all gone, and then he thanked the lady and asked her for the recipe for the scones and the cream.

Then he set off back home, put the blue boots away in the blue cupboard, and that night, for the first time in three days, he went to bed with a full belly.

Of course, being a giant, the next morning he was hungry again, so he went downstairs.

'I am Giant Grumble,
You can hear my tummy rumble!'

'Yes, I can!' said his mother. 'Good morning! What would you like for breakfast, Giant Grumble?'

'I want porridge, please!'

'Of course you can, Giant Grumble,' said his mother. She looked very happy. She served him up a great steaming bowl of porridge, and when Giant Grumble had finished, he gave his mother the recipe for the scones and clotted cream, and you can probably guess what they had for tea later on that afternoon!

This story is based on a tale told to me by Dorothy Coombes of Portesham. The West Country of England and Lebanon are both places where clotted cream is made and enjoyed.

6

The Drowners

The Drowners

The Valley of the River Frome has lots of water meadows: low-lying fields beside a river, that have streams and ditches running through them. In past times, the farmers used to flood the fields from time to time, which helped the grass to grow and provide good grazing for the cattle. You can still see the remains of the old hatches and channels that irrigated and controlled the water levels in the meadows. Rivers and streams are wonderful places to play, but you always have to be very careful and respectful of water, and maybe that's why this story came about. It was told to me by Sue Worth, who grew up in Stratton near Dorchester, in the middle of water meadow country. Sue was told the story when she was at school.

HAVE YOU EVER seen a really beautiful person? Someone so extraordinarily attractive that all you can do is stare at them? A one-in-a-million sort of person? Imagine that you saw two of them, what are the chances of that? Suppose you saw three, or four, seven or eight – early in the morning it would be, when no one else was about, or in the evening, just after the sun had gone down, but while there was still light in the sky.

That's what the Drowners are like. A sparkle on the water, a splash in the ripples from a trout rising to take a mayfly – and there they are, looking at you. Their clothes shimmer, the rings on their fingers flash, and their eyes call to you.

'Come on,' they say, 'don't be shy! Look what we have for you'.

Across the water meadow. Across the stream. Peeping through the yellow flags and the water sedge, where the Frome twists and the old hatch gate is stuck open. They have jewels on their clothes, on their wrists, on the fingers that beckon, and your head whirls and your mouth gawps, and your feet are somehow fixed, sinking in the cold mud on the edge of the water.

There are long-horned cattle in the distance, grazing unconcernedly in the lush grass beyond the streams. Birds fly across the sky, silhouetted against the clouds, but there's no sound. Nothing except the splash of the water and the chink, chink of the jewels on the long fingers of the Drowners. Their hands move slowly, they beckon. They reach under the surface of the stream and bring out long ribbons, chains of precious stones so bright that the colours flash in your eyes across the water.

'Come on, these are for you.' Did they speak, or did you just want to imagine that you'd heard them say those words? 'These are for you; come and get them.'

You try to move. It's muddy, cold. The water's around your ankles. Don't be stupid.

But there are coins too. They have green leather bags, green as the water mint. They're pouring the coins into the river, one by one, a stream of silver and gold, flashing circles disappearing into the mist that's rising on the water. If only you could get just a few of those coins, think what mother could do with that money.

Listen: 'These are for you; these are for you.'

Hold onto that withy. It's not so far. Look into their eyes.

'Come on, don't be shy! These are for you. Reach out. It's not deep, it's not deep, it's not so deep …

'MARY HALLETT! COME HOME AT ONCE!'

And they're gone. Just like that. The Drowners are gone. The Frome runs on, swirling and bubbling through the water meadows, and you can look all day long but you'll see no sign of those coins on the river bed, or the jewelled fingers and beautiful smiles of the Drowners in the reed beds. And a good job too!

7

Where's the Hare?

Old Joe Brown said, 'Do I dare,
To go into the country to look for a hare?
To look for a hare? To look for a hare?
To go into the country to look for a hare?'

He hurried from the house and he stumbled in the stubble,
The hare's in the hedgerow, keeping out of trouble.
Keeping out of trouble, keeping out of trouble,
The hare's in the hedgerow, keeping out of trouble.

He walked past the wheat and he looked in the copse,
The hare's in the gorse bush, learning how to box!
Learning how to box! Learning how to box!
The hare's in the gorse bush, learning how to box!

He searched in the valley and he looked in the spring,
The hare's on the hillside, watching everything.
Watching everything, watching everything,
The hare's on the hillside, watching everything.

He puffed up the path, he came to the stile,
The hare's in the undergrowth, watching all the while.
Watching all the while, watching all the while,
The hare's in the undergrowth, watching all the while.

He scrambled to the ridge, and he looked out to sea,
The hare's right behind him, underneath a tree.
Underneath a tree, underneath a tree,

The hare's right behind him underneath a tree.

He walked all day and he walked all night,
The hare's in the moonlight, laughing at the sight.
Laughing at the sight, laughing at the sight,
The hare's in the moonlight, laughing at the sight.

When Joe got home his wife said, 'Where have you been Joe?' He said, 'I went to see the hare.
I went to see the hare, I went to see the hare,
I went to see the hare, but the hare wasn't there!'

8

Jack and the Boat

Jack and the Boat

DO YOU KNOW Jack? He was the one who climbed up the Beanstalk and stole the golden goose from the giant. But what you might not know was that Jack had two brothers, Bill and Tom, and the three of them were always trying to outdo each other; and because Jack was the youngest, he had to be clever to outdo the strength of his older brothers.

However, one thing that they all agreed was that they wanted to be fishermen. One day they went to their mother and asked her to buy them a boat.

'A boat?' she said. 'I can't afford to buy a boat for you boys! If you want a boat, you'll have to make it yourselves, go up to the woods and cut down trees. But I am going to help you. I'm going to bake three special buns each for you boys, and those buns will be full of energy so you can work all day in the woods chopping down trees. In return, you must promise me you'll eat the buns.'

Well, the three of them did promise, and the following morning up goes Tom to the woods with an axe and a saw. Tom was the eldest and Tom was the strongest, and by lunchtime he'd cut down five great trees. Tom sat on the trunk of the biggest tree, had a cup of tea and began to eat one of the special buns his mother had made for him. He was just about to sink his teeth into the second bun when he noticed a very old lady sitting on the end of the tree trunk. The Old Lady looked at Tom and spoke.

'Well done, Tom!' she said. 'That's good work; you must be very strong to cut down so many trees. Can you spare me one of those buns you're eating?'

Well, Tom remembered what his mother had said, so he replied, 'I'm really sorry, I can't. I promised my mother I would eat them, for energy. I've got a lot of work to do here.'

'That doesn't matter, Tom. That's fine, but you will get your reward,' said the Old Lady, and then she just disappeared, which was strange. Tom finished off the buns, sharpened up his axe and went back into the woods. He chose a great tall tree and swung his axe at it, but the tree shattered just as if it was made of glass.

So did the next one and the next. In the end, he gave up and went home and told his mother what had happened.

'Well, never mind. Let's see how Bill gets on tomorrow,' she said, and Bill gave a lopsided grin and reckoned it wouldn't be hard to do better than Tom, and Tom just glared.

Early next morning, up went Bill to the woods, and at first he was cautious. He didn't want to get cut by any glass trees! But it was fine, the trees had all turned back to wood.

All morning Bill worked away. By lunchtime there were four more great trees laid on the ground alongside the five that Tom had felled the previous day. Bill sat on one and had a cup of tea. He began to eat one of the special buns his mother had made for him. He was just about to sink his teeth into the second bun, when he noticed the Old Lady, sitting on the end of the tree trunk. The Old Lady looked at Bill and spoke.

'Well Bill, that's pretty good work; you must be very strong to cut down so many trees. Can you spare me one of those buns you're eating?'

Bill remembered what his mother had said, so he replied, 'I'm really sorry, I can't. I promised mother I would eat them, for energy. I've got a lot of work to do here, there's a boat to be built.'

'Don't worry, that doesn't matter at all Bill. That's fine, but you will get your reward,' replied the Old Lady, and then she just disappeared, which was strange. Bill finished off the buns, sharpened up his axe and went back into the woods.

He chose a great tall tree and swung his axe at it, but this time it didn't shatter like glass – this time his axe jumped back at him and the whole tree rang like a bell. He tried another and another, but it was no good: every tree in the wood had turned into hard iron and all Bill did was to blunt his axe. In the end, there was nothing to do but go home and tell his mother what had happened.

'Well then, it's all down to Jack!' said his mother. Tom and Bill just laughed, because to tell you the truth, Jack was the smallest and the weakest of the three brothers. It was all he could do to drag the axe up to the woods. When he finally got there he was very careful, because he didn't want to blunt the axe on an iron tree or get cut by a glass tree. But all was well, the trees had turned back to wood again.

All morning, Jack hacked away at a slender little tree until, just before lunch, he managed to bring it down. He sat on that tree, had a cup of tea and began to eat one of his mother's buns. He was just about to sink his teeth into the second bun, when he noticed the Old Lady, sitting on the end of the tree trunk. She looked at Jack and spoke.

'Well Jack, that's quite a good tree! Can you spare me one of those buns you're eating?'

Jack looked at the Old Lady, and he felt sorry for her. He felt pretty full himself already, so he thought that really, it wouldn't hurt to give one of the buns to her. So that's what he did and the two of them sat there, munching away until the buns were all finished.

'Now Jack, you helped me and I'll help you. What are you doing? Why have you cut down all these trees?'

Then Jack told the Old Lady all about the boat, and how he and his bothers wanted to be fishermen.

'Well, what do you have to do?' she asked. 'How do you turn these trees into a boat?'

'First of all, you have to split the trees. Then you make them into planks. Next, you lay the keel and fit on the ribs, and then you shape the sides of the boat. It's hard work and it's skilled work!'

'Right, Jack,' said the Old Lady. 'You go into the woods and cut down one more tree for the mast and I'll see what I can do.'

Jack thought to himself that it was not very likely that an old lady would be much help at boat-building, but he kept that thought to himself. He did as the Old Lady suggested and went off to cut down another tree.

When he came back a couple of hours later, there, in the middle of the wood, was the complete framework of a wooden boat – keel, ribs and all!

'Wow, that's amazing!' Jack could hardly believe his eyes.

'What's next?' asked the Old Lady.

'Well, you have to nail the planks on the ribs, put on the deck, step the mast, raise the spars, rig the ropes, tie up the sails, put the anchor on the bow and the wheel astern.'

'Alright, Jack,' said the Old Lady. 'You just cut down one smallish tree for a flagpole, and I'll see what I can do. Don't be long!'

Off went Jack into the woods. It didn't take him more than half an hour to cut down a flagpole tree. But if Jack worked fast, the Old Lady worked faster!

When he came back, he was astonished to see that the boat was finished – planks, decks, masts, rigging and sails all in place and shipshape.

'It's fabulous, thank you so much!'

'What's next?' asked the Old Lady.

'The only thing left to do is to paint the boat.'

The Old Lady gave Jack a paintbrush.

'Thank you, but I shall need paint,' he said.

'Just try it, Jack!'

When Jack touched the paintbrush on the side of the boat, a red stripe came out! When he'd walked right round, the colour changed to yellow, then blue, then green, then purple, then gold, until that boat looked like a rainbow.

'It's a very special boat,' said Jack. 'There's just one problem.'

'What's the problem?' asked the Old Lady.

'The problem is that this boat is in the

middle of a wood, fifteen miles from the sea. How are going to get her into the water?'

Then the Old Lady stood and laughed, until the whole wood rang with laughter.

'Jack,' she said, 'this boat is a magic boat. If you get in and sing that old sailor song, "Hooray and Up She Rises", she will rise up and fly North, East, West or South. She can go under the sea like a submarine, or up into the sky like a spaceship. She can even go back into the past or forwards into the future – wherever you tell her to go!'

Jack was speechless. He just stared at the boat.

'But if ever you want to land, Jack, you must say this special word: 'Pitch!' And the boat will come down and you can get off to explore.'

Then Jack thanked the Old Lady, got into the boat and straight away he set off on his adventures.

Jack loved flying through the clouds. He loved looking down as the countries passed beneath him. After a while, he saw a beautiful castle. He'd always wanted to visit a castle, so he said 'Pitch!' and down went the magic boat. It landed in the castle moat. The King rushed out and shook Jack by the hand.

'Jack, that's the best boat I've ever seen!' exclaimed the King. 'In fact, you're such a fine fellow I'd like you to marry my beautiful daughter!'

Just then, out came the beautiful daughter.

'I'm not going to marry Jack just because he has a painted boat,' she said. 'I'll only marry him if he can play a decent hornpipe on a melodeon!'

Poor Jack was in despair at that, because he didn't even have a melodeon, let alone know how to play one. But then he remembered he was in a magic boat, and he looked under the seat and sure enough, there was a melodeon. He took out the instrument and found he could play it straight away! And the Princess began to laugh, and then she began to dance. She danced down the steps of the castle, across the drawbridge and into the boat. The two of them flew off, and together they had many more extraordinary adventures.

But even that wasn't quite the end of the story. After a few months, Jack began to get homesick. He thought how much he would like to see his mother again.

'Cheer up, Jack,' said the Princess. 'Don't forget, this is a magic boat. Wherever you want to be, it will take you there!' And sure enough when Jack looked down, there was his mother's house, and there was Bill and Tom and his mother standing by the stream waving.

Together, Jack and the Princess shouted 'Pitch!' Down went the magic boat and landed in the stream. Bill and Tom came up, hauled Jack out of the boat (the Princess got out too) and they clambered in.

'Right then, Jack,' said Tom. 'Now it's our turn! How do you make this boat fly?'

'It's easy,' answered Jack. 'You just sing "Hooray and Up She Rises", and off you go!' So Bill and Tom began to sing, and off they went, up into the sky! However, Bill and Tom had been too hasty – they'd forgotten to ask how to make the boat come down. So as far as we know, they are still flying around in the magic boat to this very day!

'Welcome home!' said Jack's mother. 'And I'm very pleased to meet you too, my dear. Come on in, both of you, tea's ready!'

Jack's mother got out a tin table and piled it high with food and drink; but she put so much on the table that

The tin table bended,
So this story's ended.

I first heard a version of this story in Newfoundland, Canada. It was collected from a storyteller called William Pitman, who called it 'Jack and the Beautiful Punt'. There are very strong links between Dorset and Newfoundland, based on the cod fishing that used to take place on the Grand Banks. Poole was the centre for the trade in Dorset. Several merchant families in the town ran big enterprises that involved fleets of ships, large warehouses and a triangular trade that sent vessels, men and stores to Newfoundland. The cod was dried and salted, packed into barrels, and taken south to European countries, particularly Italy and Spain. The final leg of the journey was to bring back olive oil, wine and salt from the Mediterranean countries. Newfoundlanders trace their ancestry to three main sources: Dorset, Devon and Ireland. There are communities in Newfoundland where Dorset surnames such as Pitman are common, and you can still hear recognisably West Country accents.

9
The Map

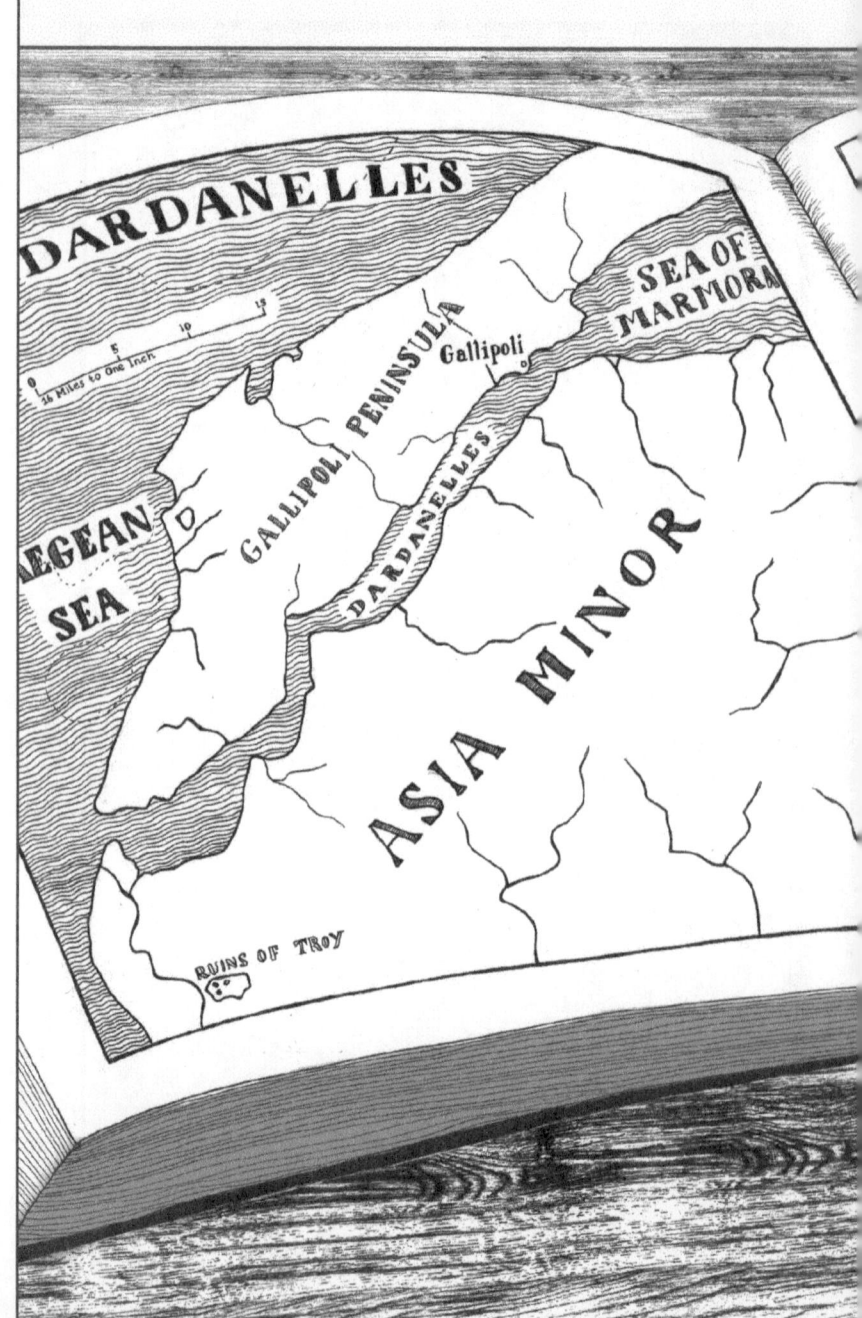

The Map

REUBEN LOVED TO draw. To sit down with a clean white page in front of him and to make lines, shapes and patterns appear was a kind of magic that he could weave for himself. He'd lean against a tree and stare at the animals in the fields at Foxholes Farm and the birds up in the trees, and then he would capture their likeness on the paper. There was never any mistaking Reuben's animals – you could almost have heard his pigs grunt, his horses practically galloped off the page, and his sheep oozed sheepiness. Every one of his drawings in his school exercise book had *very good* marked against it. There was no doubt at all that Reuben Hansford could draw.

But even greater than his love of drawing was his fascination with maps. Hung up on the walls of the tiny schoolroom in Littlebredy were brightly coloured maps of the world, and every one of them promised adventure and excitement. The long map of the Americas, with the great plains and deep snows of Canada at the top, and in the middle the prospect of opportunity, freedom and riches for all in the great United States. How impressive and full of promise that name sounded! The cactuses, cowboys and Spanish speakers in Mexico, and then the colourful, exotic, unexplored riches of South America at the bottom, which he would reach by sailing on a windjammer around Cape Horn in the ice and snow. At last his journey would end and he would arrive, blinking in the morning sunlight, in Valparaiso Bay …

Every country came alive in Reuben's imagination. He studied the maps, and then drew them for himself in his drawing book. One by one, the countries were captured, until the whole round world was pressed flat in Reuben's book. So many lands, peoples and stories! It was a wonder that the book didn't push up the lid of his desk and burst out, filling the entire schoolroom with a multitude of faces, voices, songs and stories.

Best of all he loved the map of the Dardanelles. The eastern end of the

Mediterranean Sea, the Gateway to the East, surrounded on one side by the bible lands that he heard about every Sunday at Sunday School. Greece, Italy and Turkey; the ancient world, the cradle of civilisation, the source of so many legends and stories, languages and lives.

What if Odysseus, sailing his glittering vessel through the straits of the Dardanelles and ignoring the call of the Sirens that would drive him onto the rocks, should suddenly have need of more crew and call out, 'Reuben! Come on board, Reuben!'

Crash! A board ruler came down on the desktop, inches away from the Dardanelles.

'Reuben Hansford! Daydreaming again? Write out twenty times:

> Tell me not, in mournful numbers,
> 'Life is but an empty dream!'
> For the soul is dead that slumbers,
> And things are not what they seem.

Reuben reluctantly closed his drawing book, but as he did, he sneaked one more look at his favourite map and a name seemed to reach out to him: Gallipoli.

'I'll go there,' he said to himself. 'I'll go there soon.'

Ten years later, Reuben's wish came true in a very unexpected way. A war was coming, and soldiers were needed again. The schoolboy had become a strong young man, well used to farm work, horses and outdoor life. He followed the advice of family friends and joined the Dorset Yeomanry. After training in Norfolk, the regiment were ordered overseas, and Reuben found himself on a troopship bound for Egypt. It was strange to be on such a large ship for the first time, but Reuben enjoyed it. After all, he was still looking after horses, even though he was at sea!

'I've started my travels,' he wrote home. 'We're bound for Egypt.'

After several weeks at sea they arrived at their destination, and they set up camp by the River Nile. They trained for months. One night, in April 1915, the sergeant gathered his men around a large map. He pointed out their destination.

'Anyone know where this is?' he asked.

Rueben replied at once, 'It's Gallipoli, sir, in the Dardanelles – the gateway to Constantinople.'

'Bright lad,' said the Sergeant approvingly. 'Aye, that's where we're bound for, and if we Yeomanry don't show the Turks a thing or two, my name's not George Rogers! One thing though – we're not taking the horses. Where we're going, horses won't be any good.'

For the first time, Reuben felt uneasy. He'd never known a time or place where a horse might not be useful. But at least there was no danger of the horses getting hurt …

And so it was that Reuben came ashore that night with the foot soldiers, dug a hasty trench and tried to sleep under a great, dark sky of unfamiliar stars. All around him, he heard the constant noise of insects and saw the tiny flickerings of lanterns and camp fires along the beach, into the foothills below the great cliffs of Gallipoli.

'Never mind,' he thought to himself. 'I'm here to play my part, it doesn't matter if it's not quite what I expected. I've still done it – I've got to Gallipoli!'

'Now then, Hansford. What's this? Can't sleep?' said Sergeant Rogers.

'No, sir, I'm too excited. I've always wanted to come to Gallipoli!'

'Blimey!' said the sergeant, shaking his head. 'You're a strange one. Me, I'd rather be back in Bristol or London, or anywhere but here. What's so special about Gallipoli?'

'I drew it on a map when I was at school. I dreamt that one day I'd be here, and now I am. I want to go to San Francisco and Valparaiso and Canton, and –'

'Travel the world eh? Well, we've a job to do here first, but I wish you luck my lad and I truly hope you get to see all the places on your maps. Now, goodnight!'

A few days later Reuben was badly wounded, and he died on the way home on a hospital ship in the Mediterranean. His name is remembered on the war memorial in the churchyard at Littlebredy. The verse in this story comes from A Psalm of Life *by H.W. Longfellow, which Reuben copied into his schoolbook. Reuben Hansford's letters and books can be seen in the Military Museum at the Castle Keep in Dorchester.*

10

Jack with a Lantern

Jack with a Lantern, Jack with a light,
He'll lead you astray on a cold winter's night,
So give him a sup, and give him his pay,
Or Jack with a Lantern will lead you astray

The farmer was worried. His shepherd was getting old, and who would replace him? For years, Old Jacob had tended the flock on Higher Farm, and the farmer knew he could trust him to get on with his job. Jacob, for his part, loved his work and did what was required and more for the flock.

Of course, he didn't do it on his own: he relied on his black and white collie Fan – 'Best dog I've ever had,' he'd say. And if you'd been out in Long Meadow when Fan was rounding up the sheep, creeping up on them so as not to frighten them, gently turning them and steering them to the pens, or wherever Jacob wanted them to go, then you would have said, 'That's a good sheepdog, for sure.'

But, as I told you, Jacob was getting old. It was harder to put on his heavy coat and go out in the rain and the frost on a winter's night to see to the sheep. Bending down to pick up a newborn lamb, he felt his back more than he used to. The winter cold seemed to creep into his bones much sooner, and it seemed to stay much longer than invited! Fan, too, was a little slower, her coat a little greyer – still willing, but somehow not so sharp and eager.

One afternoon in October, when the leaves were on the turn and the first frosts were just around the corner, the farmer took Jacob aside.

'You've been a good shepherd for me Jacob, and you know how much I value what you do, but you can't go on forever. What can we do about finding someone to replace you?'

Jacob smiled. 'Great minds think alike!' he said. 'Young George Annett down in the village – I've had my eye on him for some time. That dog of his will be useful. Too rash and tearaway now of course, but that's how young chaps are. That's how they should be.

No one ever learned anything without making mistakes! He's full of enthusiasm and quick to learn. That quad bike of his is a horrible, noisy thing; you wouldn't see me dead on one of 'em! Give me my old Land Rover any day! But I reckon if you were to take George on, he'd turn into a decent shepherd within a couple of years.'

'I don't know, Jacob. It's a responsible job and he's very young …'

'Well, sir, get him up for a trial. Let's see what he can do.'

George Annett was delighted when the farmer asked him to come up that Saturday. Jacob had put a small flock in Upper Meadow, and George and his dog Tan set to work. George revved up the quad bike, whistled and shouted, and the dog ran off at top speed, yelping at the heels of the sheep.

The sheep were in a right tizzy. They scattered around the field, not knowing which way to turn. More whistles, more yelps. Tan circled them, drove them into the pen and sat triumphant, while the sheep bleated and panted, dizzy and bewildered.

'There you are, sir, nothing to it!' said George, patting his dog.

'What d'you think, Jacob?' said the farmer.

'Well, he was quick. I can't deny that. But too much hurry, too much worry, too much push. Gently does it with sheep.'

'Will you teach him, Jacob? Stay on until he's ready to take over?'

'Yes, sir. If he's prepared to learn, I'm prepared to teach.'

The farmer turned to George. 'Will you learn from Jacob?'

George frowned. 'I reckon Tan and me know the job already, but I suppose maybe there's one or two things he can show me.'

'Aye, maybe there is,' said Jacob, 'and your dog'll learn from old Fan too, if she's prepared to listen.'

As always, the farmer took Jacob's advice and took George and his dog on.

'It's up to you, George: learn your craft from Jacob, and you'll be the best shepherd in Dorset. Any farmer will be pleased to pay you good money for your skills.'

So that's how it was, and the two men and their dogs worked together at Higher Farm. But the younger man grew impatient at Jacob's old-fashioned ways. He was frustrated by the constant advice that he was given on the proper way to do things.

'Just because that's how it's always been done, doesn't mean it still has to be done like that,' he'd say. 'Things have moved on, Jacob, you don't need to do that anymore.'

Jacob was stubborn. 'What's right is right, what's wrong is wrong. Too much hurry, too much worry, too much push. Too much noise! Slow down, get it done right!'

And the two dogs were the same. Young Tan was always running around eager to get on, full of youthful enthusiasm; and wily old Fan, who could have rounded up the sheep with her eyes closed, was often irritated and annoyed by the younger dog.

'How are they getting on, Jacob?' asked the farmer just after Christmas, when lambing was due to begin.

'Oh, we'll get there, but I won't deny we have our moments,' said the old shepherd. 'Still too much hurry, too much worry, too much push. But we'll get there I reckon.'

That weekend, the lambing began. The sheep were all penned and hurdled for safety, and it was an all-night job for Jacob and George.

'I don't like the look of the weather,' said Jacob. 'There's snow in those clouds.' The boy looked at the weather app on his phone.

'Nothing's forecast,' he said. 'We'll be fine. Let's get done and get off home.'

As the sun went down, Jacob took a bowl and put some bread and milk into it, just as his father had done, and his father before him. George watched him with a mixture of amusement and contempt.

'Who's that for then, Jacob? The fairies?'

Jacob began to sing in a high-pitched, quavering voice:

Jack with a Lantern, Jack with a light,
He'll lead you astray on a cold winter's night,
So give him a sup, and give him his pay,
Or Jack with a Lantern will lead you astray.

He stopped singing. 'Aye, Jack watches over this shed all through lambing.'

George could hardly believe his ears. 'Fairy stories? Nursery rhymes? Do you expect me to believe that? You'll be wanting to wassail the apple trees next!'

Jacob carried out the bowl. He put it carefully on the wall behind the lambing shed.

'I've never lost a lamb here and that's thanks to Jack.'

George scoffed. 'Wasting good bread and milk every night on Jack with a Lantern!' he jeered. 'You live in the past, Jacob. Any fool can see it's the hedgehogs and badgers that eat the stuff'.

'That's how it's always been done at lambing, and as long as I'm here that's how it will be done,' said Jacob quietly.

That night, it began to snow and it kept on snowing. The electric light in the lambing shed lit up the flurries that crept into the straw, settled on the rafters and around the door. Jacob anxiously counted the ewes.

'There's three missing,' he said. 'They'll be up Long Meadow. You'd best get yourself up there and bring them back.'

'Can't you do it?' said the boy. 'I've been out four times already. You do it.'

'I asked you to go,' said the old shepherd slowly. 'If my boss had asked me to do something when I was your age, I'd have done it straight away, no questions asked.'

George was wet and cold and fed up. Jacob was tired and his whole body ached. Shepherding didn't seem such a good job on a night like this. An argument began that had been brewing for several months. At last George got up, swore at the old man and kicked at Fan as he pulled on his coat and walked out into the snow. He called to Tan, started up the quad bike and off he went.

Up on the roof of the lambing shed, Jack with a Lantern had heard every word. He looked through the window, and saw old Jacob cradling his dog.

The dog was whimpering and the old man was shaking. At last, Jacob picked himself up, took some straw and slowly began to check the ewes and lambs in the lambing shed. Jack with a Lantern put the lid on his bread and milk, wiped his mouth, and disappeared into the darkness.

George drove through the snow in a fury. He skidded in a snowdrift and came off. He managed to right the bike, and headed more slowly up the hill, looking for the ewes. The lights on the quad bike failed. He stopped and looked around. In the driving snow he couldn't see a thing, he was lost on his own farm! How stupid was that?

Then he saw a light ahead, flickering, and a voice calling out:

'Over here! Over here!'

'Must be the old man, come out to help,' he thought to himself. He drove towards the light. The light moved down the hill.

'Over here! Over here!'

'He's leading the way,' thought George, and he followed the light through the snowstorm. Tan was cowering in the back under a fertilizer sack – she didn't like the snow.

And then, just above the wind and wrapped in the snowflakes, he heard someone singing. And the song went like this:

Jack with a Lantern, Jack with a light,
He'll lead you astray on a cold winter's night,
So give him a sup, and give him his pay,
Or Jack with a Lantern will lead you astray.

Suddenly he felt the wheels of the quad bike sink and the engine stalled. Icy water lapped around his ankles, he was fast in a quag and the sheep were nowhere to be seen. The light disappeared. He cursed, but that did no good. He took out his mobile. No signal.

'Help! Help!'

No one answered. George was well and truly stuck. Up in the snow clouds, Jack with a Lantern chuckled.

'That's taught him a lesson!' he said to himself. He made his way back towards the lambing shed, dancing and dodging round the snowflakes.

Old Jacob was worried. He looked at his watch. Where was the boy? He'd been gone an hour. Shouldn't have taken more than twenty minutes. Jacob took out his mobile phone. It was practically unused, he didn't like the thing, but sometimes they did have their uses. The light from the screen lit up his tired face, squinting at the tiny buttons. No signal – must be the snowstorm.

There was nothing for it but to pull on his old mac and hat and get his torch – but the battery was dead. Jacob took down the old hurricane lamp his father had used. He found the paraffin, pumped up the pressure, trimmed the wick and lit the lamp. A warm glow filled the shed. Jacob called Fan, and together the old friends went out into the snow.

If anything, it was snowing harder. You really couldn't see more than a metre in front of your nose. But Jacob pulled his hat brim down and Fan led the way.

'Long Meadow, old girl – we'll try our luck there first.'

So off they went into the night. They found the ewes sheltering under a hawthorn by the edge of Long Meadow, and quickly got them back into a pen in the lambing shed.

'Come on, Fan, we'd better find George and Tan. Find 'em, there's a good girl, find!'

Out they went again, down the hill with Fan leading the way. At last they found George, Tan and the quad bike stuck in the quag.

'However did you get stuck down here?'

George glared. 'Followed your light, of course.'

Jacob stared at him. 'Not my light,' he said. 'I never left the hut until just now. What kind of light was it?'

George told him it was waving around, and calling out, 'Over here! Over here!'

Jacob smiled. 'That will have been Jack with a Lantern. He doesn't take kindly to folks that don't believe in him!'

'Where's the ewes?' said George. Jacob was pleased – at least he was concerned about them. 'Don't you worry,' he said. 'Me and Fan sorted them. Let's get you two back, you both look shrammed.'

'What about my bike?'

'Leave it,' said the old man. 'We'll come back in the morning with the Land Rover. It's easier to walk in this snow.'

'I don't know the way,' said George.

'I do,' said Jacob. 'So does Fan. You two follow us, and you'll be all right.'

Back they went to the lambing shed. And up on the top of the shed sat Jack with a

Lantern, eating his bread and milk, laughing quietly to himself.

After that, George wasn't quite so full of himself. He listened to Jacob's words of wisdom. Tan was never in quite such a terrible hurry, and boy and dog became better shepherds as a result of it.

When the time came for Jacob and Fan to retire, George and Tan took over and made a good job of it. Does he still put out the bread and milk for Jack with a Lantern at lambing time, like Jacob used to do? You'll have to ask him yourself!

Jack with a Lantern, Jack with a light,
He'll lead you astray on a cold winter's night,
So give him a sup, and give him his pay,
Or Jack with his Lantern will lead you astray.

Will-o'-the Wisp, Whipowill, or Jack with a Lantern is the country name for marsh fire, which can occasionally be seen at night, flickering over marshy or boggy ground.

11

The Beggar's Wedding

STORIES CAN BE songs and songs can be stories. Both are handed down from one generation to the next, until no one can quite remember who wrote the song in the first place or where the story came from. This is one of those old tales, called *The Beggar's Wedding*, or the *Dorsetshire Garland*. It begins like this:

> All you that delight in a jest that is true,
> Give ear to these lines I unfold to you …

Years and years ago, there was a famous knight in Dorsetshire. He and his wife had a beautiful baby daughter called Susannah, and she was their pride and joy. The knight's neighbour and closest friend was a rich merchant, and he and his wife were the proud parents of a tiny son. His name was Jemmy and he was exactly the same age as the knight's daughter. The knight and his wife enjoyed good health, but the merchant and his wife were both stricken with a sickness.

When the two children were only three years old, the merchant and his wife were near to death. The merchant called for his friend and he spoke earnestly to him.

'I know that we are dying,' he said. 'You are my best friend. Will you look after my young son Jemmy when we are gone, and raise him as one of your family?'

The knight promised faithfully that he would.

'Bless you,' said the dying man. 'One more thing, my dear old friend – my greatest wish would be that my son might marry your daughter Susannah. I will leave all my lands and riches to them, to make sure that they both live happily ever after.'

The knight gratefully agreed to this generous offer, but made the practical point that the merchant's son might die before reaching manhood. What should happen then?

'In that case,' said the merchant, 'all my wealth shall come to you, old friend, for the kindness that you have shown to my family and me.'

A few days later the merchant and his wife died at exactly the same time on the same day. They were buried together in one grave. The knight took Jemmy into his own household, and for a few years he honoured his dead friend's memory, looking after the boy as if he was his own son.

The years went past and Jemmy and Susannah grew up together. They were best friends and they were inseparable. Their delight in each other's company was plain to see, and the beauty of both children impressed everyone. But gradually, the knight began to think that perhaps his daughter was too beautiful and too high-born to marry a merchant's son. Then he convinced himself that not only would it be a misfortune for his daughter, it was his duty as a responsible parent to make a better match for Susannah. The knight became completely obsessed with this idea. At last, he resolved to have Jemmy killed so that he could claim the merchant's money and allow his daughter to marry a more suitable husband.

It happened that a tribe of beggars came into Dorset shortly afterwards, which gave the knight his opportunity. He sent his manservant to seek out a beggar who might be prepared to assist a gentleman, no questions asked. The reward would be a large sum of money. A beggar was duly found, sworn to secrecy, and told what to do.

The following day, the knight walked out into the garden where Jemmy and Susannah were happily playing together. He invited the boy to come for a walk with him. Susannah wanted to come too, but her father said no and sent her indoors. Then the knight called in the beggar, who was dressed in fine clothes so as not to arouse the boy's suspicions.

'This is my manservant, John,' said the knight. 'He will take you for a walk and show you many fine things, and then later on you can play with Susannah again.'

So Jemmy did what he was told, and went off with the disguised beggar. They walked for many miles, the child innocently chattering away. The further they walked, the more the beggar grew to like the boy. After a while, Jemmy began to miss his playmate and asked the beggar where they were going. The beggar couldn't bring himself to kill the child, so he decided instead to take the child back to his wife Doll to raise as their own.

When Doll saw the boy and heard the tale she was delighted.

'He's a good-looking boy!' she said. 'I like him, he can go a-begging with us!'

At first the boy was happy in his strange new home, but soon he began to pine for Susannah. The beggar decided that it would be natural justice if he was to steal her too, and bring her back to live with his family.

One dark night he crept up to the knight's hall, and carried off the sleeping girl in a blanket. Along the road Doll was waiting. She stripped off Susannah's fine clothes, flung them over a hedge and dressed her as a beggar. By daybreak they were miles away, hidden amongst the community of beggars, and Jemmy was reunited with Susannah.

When the knight found his daughter was gone, he was desolate. He offered a reward of Five thousand pounds to anyone who could find the girl, but all that could be found were her clothes, discarded in a field, which convinced the knight that his Susannah was dead.

Then the greedy knight wept for the loss of his child.

'This is all my own fault,' he said to himself. 'I have brought this misfortune upon myself. I dared to take a life for my own purposes and now I have lost Susannah, the joy of my heart.'

Meanwhile, far away, Jemmy and Susannah were happy together with their new parents. Although the beggars had very few possessions, they were rich in other ways: they had songs, stories, music and friendship. With their beautiful looks and pleasant ways, the children were very successful as beggars, and the beggar and his wife were delighted.

One morning the beggar spoke to his wife.

'Doll,' he said, 'I've had an idea. The money I was paid to kill Jemmy shall become a wedding gift for him and I will give twice as much again. When the two of them are eighteen they shall be married in the finest beggar's wedding that ever was known!'

Doll was so delighted with this plan that she clapped her hands, kissed her husband and declared it was the best idea he'd ever had.

'Yes,' said the beggar, 'and we'll have twenty handsome beggars to accompany Jemmy as his groomsmen, and we'll give out the news that there's to be a real beggar's wedding, and we'll do it in Dorchester.'

'Perfect,' said Doll. 'We'll have the finest food and drink!'

'Yes,' replied the beggar, 'and if the knight is still living, he can come along. I'll make him a present of his daughter once she's lawfully wed to Jemmy, which no man can put asunder!'

Doll was so excited she could hardly wait, but as the children were only ten years old, she had no choice!

For eight years they rambled all over the West Country, begging as they went.

At last the day of the wedding arrived. The whole tribe were determined to make it the best wedding ever seen. Money was found in pots and kettles. They dug up buried boxes and bags. Fine clothes were bought for bride and groom, and the clothes made even finer by sewing on gold and silver coins all over, until they shone like the stars.

A great procession was formed. First came the bride and groom in front, then the attendants, and finally all the rest of the begging tribe behind. In this way they sang and danced their way into Dorset, and all the time news of the wedding spread far and wide.

As the party came into Dorchester great crowds assembled, amazed at the beauty and splendour of bride and groom, and their outlandish attendants and guests. The beggars requested food and drink for the wedding feast, and great quantities of Blue Vinney cheese, good back-bacon and barrels of ale were freely donated. The finest and largest room in the town was hired so that as many as possible could see the wedding, and the seats were quickly taken; everyone wanted to see the beggar's wedding.

The knight was now an old man, gloomy and sad. His wife had died some years before and his life was empty. But he heard his servants talking about the beggar's wedding, so he called his man to saddle his horse and set off for Dorchester to see the spectacle.

When the knight came into the hall, the wedding ceremony and feast were already over. Jemmy and Susannah were man and wife, the food was all eaten and the drink nearly gone. The fiddles were playing, the bride and her friends were dancing in a circle. The hall shook with joy and laughter and even the sad old knight felt his spirits lift.

He looked idly at the laughing bride and something about her sent a shiver through him. He thought he recognised her, but he couldn't be sure. Then the bride got up to dance and Doll called on the fiddlers for a jig, which Susannah danced with such grace that the entire company were transfixed. Then the beggar, bursting with pride and not to be outdone, called on the musicians for a hornpipe for his son Jemmy.

'My friends,' he cried. 'A health to the bridegroom! Though he's a beggar's son brought up, he's a merchant's son by birth!'

Then the knight, his heart pounding, stepped up to the bride. He bowed low and begged her to listen to him.

'If you have the mark of a rose on your arm, I declare that you are my only daughter, who for thirteen years I have thought dead.'

The whole room was silent. Susannah and Jemmy stood stock still, staring at the knight. Then the old man fell on his knees, confessed what he'd done all those years ago and begged their pardon. He promised that he would receive them kindly if they would come to his hall, and invited the whole company to come to see that he kept his word.

For a long time, nobody spoke. Then the young couple looked at each other and smiled.

'All's well that ends well!' they said, and they took the old knight by the hand, raised him up and embraced him.

The beggars ran through the town, shouting the joyful news that true love and virtue had triumphed, and the whole of Dorchester praised the beggar who had saved the boy's life.

People say 'forgive and forget' and that's what Susannah and Jemmy did, but the old knight could never quite forget the wicked deed he'd planned to do. Not long afterwards he died, leaving the young couple six thousand pounds a year for life. Old Doll and her husband went to live with Jemmy and Susannah, and as far as we know they all lived happily ever after.

Of all the trades in England, begging is the best;
For when a beggar's tired, he can lay him down to rest,
And a-begging I will go, and a-begging I will go.

12

Granny Parsons and the Dorset Dumplings

EVERYBODY IN DORCHESTER knew Granny Parsons. She'd run her little pie shop in High East Street for as long as anyone could remember, and the quality of her pies and cakes was legendary. No one who tasted one of Granny's lardy cakes could ever eat another sort again – they were superb, unrivalled, unbeatable. The same applied to her pies and biscuits. In fact, everything she made was top quality – except for her dumplings. Granny Parsons couldn't make dumplings for toffee! They looked disgusting, they smelt disgusting, they tasted disgusting and they were disgusting! All those things might not have mattered quite so much if they'd been light and feathery – but Granny's dumplings were hard. They were solid. They were heavy as lead.

How such a wonderful cook could produce such appalling dumplings was a puzzle. And why people continued to buy them was another puzzle. But the reason was that Dorchester folk are a generous lot and they didn't want to hurt Granny's feelings. So, out of the kindness of their hearts, they continued to buy the dumplings. They even came back for more. But don't worry, they didn't eat them – they used them for other purposes.

Some people used them to keep their doors open. Some people tied ropes round them and then used them to stop their roofs blowing away. Old Walter Northover the builder used them instead of flints on the front of his buildings. He created beautiful patterns with the dumplings and invented a style of decorative architecture very popular amongst the dwellers at Poundbury Camp, known affectionately as 'Nouveau-dumpling'.

Marian Moule used them as weights for all the woollen looms in her workshop. When an attacking army besieged the town and the ammunition ran out, Granny's dumplings were fired from the cannons and soon had the enemy in retreat. When a terrible storm swept away most of the Chesil Bank,

Granny's dumplings saved the day and you can still see them there, if you stand outside the Cove Inn on a stormy night.

All this might have been lost in the mists of time and the ancient chronicles of Dorset, if it wasn't for the dragon. Oh yes, the dragon! Most places suffered from occasional dragon infestations from time to time in the good old days, and Dorchester was no different.

One bright moonlit night in midsummer, George Caddy was out walking his dog by the River Frome, when he heard a great flapping sound and a whistling that also seemed to be a hissing and a screeching all in one.

'Hello,' said George to himself. 'That's not a heron.'

George was right. He turned round just in time to see a great green dragon with raggedy wings, yellow claws and staring red eyes. Fire was coming out of its nostrils.

George's dog bristled. She barked loudly at the dragon. The dragon let out a terrible roar, shot up into the air, turned over into a dive and buried itself deep in the marshes by the river under Poundbury Camp.

George high-tailed it into the town and ran from inn to tavern and from tavern to inn, telling everyone the shocking news. Mostly they laughed at him and told him to jump in the Frome, but in the end they all agreed to come down to look for George's dragon. They stared across the marsh. There was nothing to see. They went out with sticks and prodded the ground. Nothing. They brought trumpets and drums and made as much noise as they could. Still nothing.

'Seems to me George Caddy has been pulling our leg!' said Charlie Chant. 'And I reckon we should throw him in the Frome!'

'Good idea!' shouted the crowd. They grabbed George to throw him into the river, but just at that moment the marsh erupted, a terrible pong filled the air and with a ghastly shriek the dragon emerged. She swept up a whole field of cows belonging to Elspeth Swann, gobbled them down with a terrible crunching of bones and then set fire to a row of houses and a church with her awful breath.

That was just the beginning of Dorchester's dragon trouble. Sometimes the dragon would sleep for days on end, and all that could be seen was foul-smelling green bubbles that rose from the swamp. But at least once a week, she would become hungry – then she went on the rampage, and no cow, sheep or even horse was safe. It got so bad that she even tried to eat a column of soldiers who were marching into the town, and they only just escaped with their lives.

At last the townsfolk could stand it no longer. They marched to the Town Hall and demanded action.

The Mayor of Dorchester at that time was Gabriel Gwillett. He was a very timid man. He was frightened by the mice in his kitchen and terrified by the spiders in his bedroom. He once found a moth in his Mayoral robe and fainted in the council chamber. He was not the best man to fight a dragon!

'We want action!' shouted the crowd.

'Good people, what would you like me to do?' inquired the Mayor. 'Removing dragons is not something I've ever been called upon to do. I'm afraid I don't even know where to begin.'

Just then the Mayor felt someone tugging at his sleeve. He looked down and saw a girl and a boy, both aged about nine years old.

'What do you want?' inquired the Mayor. 'I'm afraid I'm rather busy at the moment, can you come back another day?'

The children shook their heads. They motioned to him to kneel down. They whispered in his ears, one on one side and the other on the other. The Mayor's eyes opened wide. He began to smile. Then he began to chuckle. And finally, he threw his Mayoral hat up in the air and began to dance a hornpipe in the street!

'He's gone crackers!' said the Town Clerk. 'Send for the town trolley and take him home as quickly and as quietly as possible!'

'STOP!' shouted the Mayor. 'Stop! Stop, I say! STOP!'

Everyone was amazed. They'd never heard the Mayor shout so loud. They all waited to see what would happen next.

'These children have had a splendid idea. They will tell you what to do. They will save our town!'

The people stared in disbelief. Two nine year olds saving the town? What could they know?

The boy spoke up. 'Go and get your carts, your wheelbarrows, your waggons and your strongest baskets. Meet us a Granny Parsons' pie shop.'

The girl spoke up. 'Come on! There's no time to waste. Do it now! RUN!'

For once, the inhabitants of Dorchester did as they were told. They fetched their waggons, carts, baskets and wheelbarrows, and filled the streets around Granny Parsons' pie shop.

'Granny, come out!' shouted the boy.

'Yes, come out!' shouted the girl. 'We need you to make as many dumplings as you can, the bigger the better. It's a matter of life and death!'

Granny looked out of her window. She saw the crowds, and their waggons and wheelbarrows, and her eyes gleamed.

'I'll need help!' she called.

At once, the troop of soldiers flung down their weapons, rolled up their sleeves and went into the pie shop. They were followed by all the milkmaids from the dairy, the milliners from the hat shop and all the prisoners from the gaol, specially released for the occasion. All afternoon, under Granny Parsons' expert instruction, they wrestled with the dumplings until at last the first batch, steaming hot, was placed into the waiting waggons.

Granny had not let them down. Those dumplings looked disgusting, they smelt disgusting, they tasted disgusting and they were disgusting! Best of all, they were as heavy as lead. It took the strongest men and women in the town, aided by the heaviest oxen and horses, to drag the waggons, baskets, carts and wheelbarrows down to the river marsh. They piled them all up in a tempting, steaming display, then ran back to the woods and waited.

Nothing happened.

They waited an hour. Still nothing happened. But just when they were about to turn on the Mayor and call him all sorts of very rude names, the marsh began to move. Horrible, noxious green bubbles rose up and burst in the air, showering everyone with foul-smelling liquid. The trees began to shake and the River Frome began to run backwards. Granny Parsons rose to the occasion.

'Come out, my little chick-a-biddy!' she yelled. 'Dinner's ready, come and get it!'

With that, the swamp erupted and the dragon shot out in a cloud of fire and stench. She rose up into the air, twisted around and then dived down towards the earth. She opened her mighty jaws, engulfed the entire heap of Granny's special recipe dumplings, and gobbled them down.

The people all held their breath.

A strange, pained expression came over the dragon's face. The corners of her gigantic mouth drooped and quivered. Her eyes began to roll and her wings began to shake and flap wildly. Then, giving the most blood-curdling, spine-chilling, breath-stopping cry of rage and despair, the dragon reared up. She tried to leap into the air to fly away. Her efforts were all in vain. The weight of Granny Parsons' Dorset dumplings pinned her to the ground. Worse than that, the marsh itself began to quiver and shake, and it wasn't long before the dragon disappeared into the swamp, dumplings and all, and was never seen again.

After that, Granny Parsons was the talk of the town. The two children were heroes. Even the Mayor was able to bask in the reflected glory of the great victory over the dragon. Granny Parsons' Dorset dumplings became famous, and they were sent all over the world in specially strengthened ships with reinforced bottoms. Some of the ships were wrecked in a great gale off the Chesil Bank and to this day, in the fiercest storms, a few of Granny's dumplings still get washed up onto the beach in amongst the seaweed and the dead crabs. If you chance to find one, don't attempt to pick it up on your own – and don't attempt to eat it. Remember what it says on the tin:

> Granny Parsons' Original Dorset Dumplings. They look disgusting, they smell disgusting, they taste disgusting, and they are disgusting!

13

The Merman

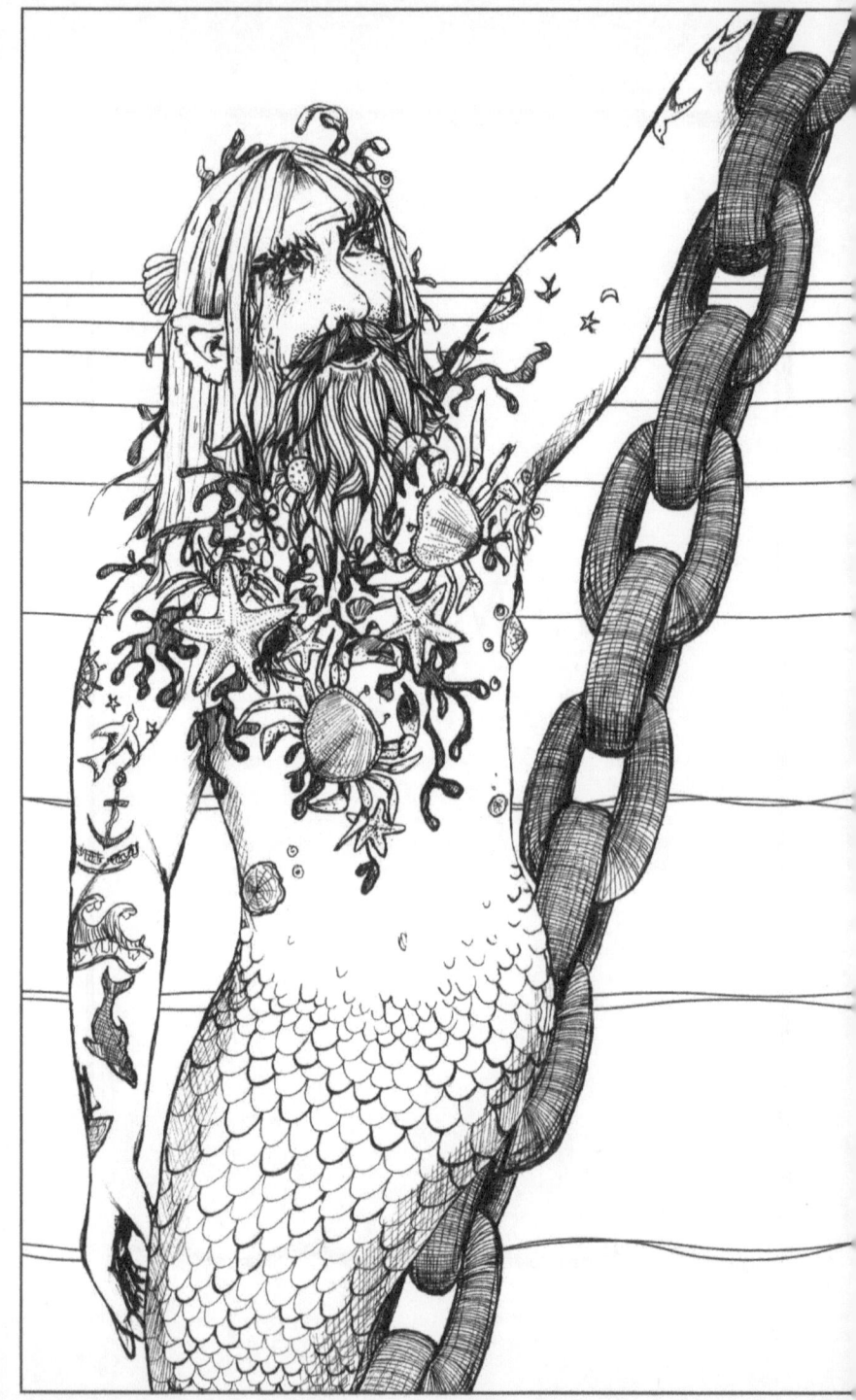

*'Twas on a summer's morning
Down cross the Southern Sea;
Our ship she lay at anchor
Waiting for a breeze …*

'Years ago,' said an old sailor, 'I was on board the *William and Nancy*, bound for the West Indies. I remember the voyage very well because of a remarkable event that occurred. I saw it with my own eyes. I'll tell you that tale now, if you will do me the honour of listening right through to the end…'

After a difficult and stormy voyage, we were very glad to reach safe harbour. The anchor was let go, and we worked all day to make the *William and Nancy* shipshape again. The crew were all looking forward to a few days ashore.

Early next morning we were awoken by a loud cry of 'man overboard!' We all ran up on deck to help. Sitting on the anchor chain, dripping from head to foot, was a man – at least, we presumed him to be a man. His hair was wild and ragged, twined with seaweed and shells. His eyes were the deepest sea blue you ever saw and his ears were red and fringed, just like the gills of a great fish. Around his throat he wore a living necklace of starfish and crabs. His upper body was coloured in deep greens and blues. His arms were covered in tattoos, just like any sailor, but the oddest thing of all was that he had no legs, only a long, scaly tail, shaped like a shark or whale. It twined itself around the anchor chain to prevent him falling back into the sea.

Every single one of us was dumbstruck by this visitor from the deep, and none of us were quite sure what to do – all except our Mate!

The Mate hailed him with a cheery welcome, bold as brass, 'What Ho!'

'And What Ho to all of ye, shipmates!' replied the merman pleasantly. 'I want a word with your Old Man if you please – I've a favour to ask, you see.'

Well, you could have knocked me down with a feather! He talked just like any other sailor! We all crowded closer to hear what he had to say, and straight away the Mate sent the cabin boy to fetch the Captain. The Captain was a man of impeccable manners, and if he was surprised to see a merman sitting on his ship's anchor, he didn't show it.

'Good afternoon, sir,' said the Captain. 'Welcome aboard the *William and Nancy*! How can we help you?'

'Well, Captain, it's like this,' began the Merman. 'You've dropped your anchor right in front of my house. You've blocked the only door. My wife's shut in and can't get out, nor my babes – and there's four of 'em!'

'Oh dear, I beg your pardon! I'm very sorry indeed. We'll haul in the anchor at once,' promised the Captain. 'Your family must be set free immediately. But my dear fellow, we're very curious to know your history! You seem to be partly a mariner like ourselves, and partly a fish! Can you tell us, please, whatever has happened to you?'

The Merman looked at us and then settled back on the anchor. 'I'd be delighted to tell you, shipmates, but I feel myself drying out, and for the likes of me, that's not good. Could one of ye turn the ship's hose on me and give me a thorough soaking before I start?'

We did exactly as he requested. We turned the firehose on him, and the salt water sparkling on his scales made a kind of rainbow all round him. You could see plainly that water was his natural element.

'Thank you kindly!' he said. 'Well now, shipmates, here's my tale.

'Many years ago, when I was a lad, I was a landsman just like yourselves. Jack Chipp, that's my name. I grew up in a small village in Dorset called Portesham, not far from the sea. At the age of twelve, I ran away to sea to join the King's Navy. A few years later I fell overboard from HMS *Hero*. It was during a terrible gale in the Bay of Biscay. I dare say you all know the spot?'

We all murmured agreement; we knew that windswept sea only too well.

'I was up aloft with several shipmates attempting to reef in the main sail, and I was blown off my perch into the waves. I sank right down to the bottom of the ocean. Right deep down into Davy Jones' Locker! I thought my number was up. But if you'll believe me, Captain, my life was saved by a girl with a fishtail!'

'Well, blow me down!' said the Captain, and the rest of us made similar colourful salty remarks, until the Mate ordered us to stow it, and let the man tell his tale.

The Merman, who had been chewing on a thick piece of bladder-wrack, cleared his throat and continued.

'Yes mates, she taught me how to live under the sea and, to cut a long story short, I made her my wife. From that day onwards my legs started to change into this flipper. So now I get my living under the sea, instead of floating on top in a British sailing vessel.'

'But do you never hanker for your old life, up aloft with the likes of we sailors?' asked the Captain.

'Oh no, Captain, I have no worries or cares down below. There's sharks of course, but there's sharks on land too, as ye all well know. But if you take care and keep a weather eye open, you come to no harm.'

'But would you like to come back to dear old England with us?' offered the Captain.

'No thank you!' replied the Merman. 'I'm happy enough where I am. It's been good to meet you all, and to yarn about old times, but I feel myself drying out again, which for the likes of me is a very bad thing. I'd be most obliged, Captain, if you'd ask your shantyman to strike up a song and get these handsome fellows to raise the anchor and set my family free.'

'Of course!' said the Captain. 'Whatever was I thinking? I'm forgetting my manners, which a Captain never ought to do. But Mr Chipp, do you have any message that we can take back to Portesham to your family? They must be very worried about you, being gone from home for so many years?'

The Merman chewed on his bladder-wrack for a moment or two.

'Aye, you can tell them at the King's Arms that you met Jack Chipp the Merman, and he had a very fishy tail to tell!'

We all laughed at that and the Cook called for three cheers for the merman. Then the Captain gave his orders:

'Mr Mate, call all hands on deck to raise the anchor!'

'Farewell then, mates,' cried the Merman, and with that he unwound his tail, gave a great flip and dived back into the sea. We all ran from the larboard to the starboard side and gazed over the edge. We were just in time to see him wave his tail before he disappeared under the water. That was the last we ever saw of Jack Chipp the Merman. We set to around the capstan, and roared out the shanty as the anchor cable creaked aboard:

Blow ye winds in the morning,
Blow ye winds Hi Ho!
Clear away your running gear,
And Blow Boys Blow!

Up came the anchor and, to our amazement, stuck on the flukes was part of a cottage roof, with a chimney pot on top – and if you'll believe me, the chimney pot was still smoking!

This curious old story exists as a sea song, and as a spoken tale. Captain Hoffman heard it told by a group of seamen on board HMS Blonde *in the West Indies in 1794.*

14

The Christmas Bull

The Christmas Bull

WILLIAM WAS THE best fiddler in the area, known all around as the man for the job when it came to dances and celebrations where music was required. So of course, when Timothy Thomas got married to Sarah Rose, it was the most natural thing in the world to ask old William to play. Now this all happened one glorious summer's day at the end of June, but to understand what happened to William, I must just make sure that you know of a very ancient old West Country belief. People say that at midnight on Christmas Eve, if you go into a stable or a barn or anywhere where farm animals are kept, you will see them on their knees in honour of the birth of Jesus. Down in Somerset they also say that at that special hour beasts can talk – but everyone knows that Somerset folk have some strange ideas.

Anyway, on the day of the wedding all the folks went to church, and there was Old William sat in the gallery, playing sacred music on the violin. Whenever the vicar called for a hymn or psalm, Old William played the tune and led the music.

When the service was over and the couple wed, the bride and groom linked arms in the traditional way and led the congregation out of the church and down towards the tithe barn. Old William walked in front playing his favourite march, which he called Bonaparte's Retreat. He'd learnt the tune from his father, who always claimed to have helped the Duke of Wellington defeat Napoleon Bonaparte at the Battle of Waterloo, and certainly he had an old gun hung over his fireplace amongst the herbs and hams.

As the procession made its way through the village, all the people came out of their houses to cheer and clap. Some of them gave small gifts to the bride and groom, and all of them gave good wishes. The sun shone, the birds sang, and everyone was in the mood for a good party!

When they finally got to the barn, it looked beautiful. The walls were freshly whitewashed, the floor was swept, there was greenery around the windows and doors. Great long tables ran down the middle of the room, all groaning with eatables and drinkables.

Everyone sat down and the feasting began – everyone except for Old William, who was perched on a barrel over to one side, playing lively song tunes and ditties to keep 'em all humming while they ate. But they didn't forget him, oh no! Because in Dorset, folk are very hospitable towards musicians; you only have to hear the twang of a fiddle or the toot of a flute and you can't help yourself, you have to dip your hand in your pocket and give them a few pence, or something to eat, or maybe a drink. So as William played someone gave him some beef, someone else gave him some cake, someone else gave him some beer and someone else gave him some cider – he was fed and watered as he played!

After two or three hours the food was all gone, so they cleared away the tables, pushed the benches to the walls, and began to dance. They did the longways dances and the circle dances, the right-hand stars and the do-si-dos; and there was Old William sawing away on the fiddle, playing Up the Sides and Down the Middle, and all the jigs and reels and hornpipes popular in that neighbourhood at the time. As he played someone gave him some more beer, and so it went on until one o'clock in the morning.

At last, when the bride and groom had gone off on honeymoon and all the guests had gone home, the only person left in the barn was Old William, absolutely exhausted – well he'd been playing all day – and, to tell you the truth, not completely sober. He was so tired that he couldn't think straight. He put his hat in his violin case and he tried to put his violin on his head! He managed to sort that out, but then he made a bigger mistake: he took a shortcut across Long Meadow.

Now, anyone in the village would have told you that Long Meadow was where the farmer kept his bull. The bull was large, fierce, and had very long horns. He was called Captain.

It's best to be careful with bulls. Normally they are fine, but they don't like being disturbed. Captain particularly disliked being disturbed at night. So when he saw William crossing his field, he decided to take action.

William was as far as he could possibly be from the four hedges, right in the middle of the field, when in the darkness he heard a pounding of hooves and the sound of heavy snorting. Looking around he saw Captain, charging towards him, horns a-glinting in the moonlight!

William was far too tired to run for it, so in the circumstances he did the only sensible thing he could: he took up his fiddle and began to play. It was very lucky for William that Captain was musical. As soon as he heard the music he stopped, listened, and a contented smile came over his face. And as long as William kept playing, all was well. As soon as he stopped to think of another tune, down went the bull's head, and his hooves were pawing the ground, so Old William had to keep on playing.

He played all his jigs and reels and hornpipes, then he played them all again. He even played a waltz or two. And the night wore on, until at last William had one of those dreadful moments that all musicians experience: you know that you know more tunes, but you can't remember what they are! And down went Captain's head, and his hooves were pawing on the ground.

Then William had a flash of inspiration, and even though it was the middle of June, he very slowly and reverently began to play and sing the old nativity hymn:

> While shepherds watched their flocks by night,
> All seated on the ground,
> The Angel of the Lord came down
> And glory shone around.

Well, it was very lucky for William that not only was Captain musical, he was also religious, and he thought it must be Christmas Eve. Down he went on his great knees, and down went his head until his horns were touching the ground.

William took his chance. He took to his heels, and was over the hedge before the bull could get up again. He always said afterwards that he'd often seen people look stupid, but he'd never seen a bull look stupid before!

And that's the story of William and the Christmas Bull.

The violin or fiddle was the favourite instrument for village music in Dorset until the arrival of melodeons and concertinas in the middle of the nineteenth century. Thomas Hardy grew up in a little cottage in Upper Bockhampton near Dorchester. He learned to play the violin and loved country dancing; his father, uncle and grandfather all played string instruments, and formed the nucleus of the church band in Stinsford parish church just outside Dorchester. Hardy loved stories, and learnt many old country tales, including this one from his grandmother. He was fascinated with stories connected to fiddles and fiddle playing, and included them in many of his poems and novels.

Society for Storytelling

Since 1993, The Society for Storytelling has championed the ancient art of oral storytelling and its long and honourable history – not just as entertainment, but also in education, health, and inspiring and changing lives. Storytellers, enthusiasts and academics support and are supported by this registered charity to ensure the art is nurtured and developed throughout the UK.

Many activities of the Society are available to all, such as locating storytellers on the Society website, taking part in our annual National Storytelling Week at the start of every February, purchasing our quarterly magazine Storylines, or attending our Annual Gathering – a chance to revel in engaging performances, inspiring workshops, and the company of like-minded people.

You can also become a member of the Society to support the work we do. In return, you receive free access to Storylines, discounted tickets to the Annual Gathering and other storytelling events, the opportunity to join our mentorship scheme for new storytellers, and more. Among our great deals for members is a 30% discount off titles from The History Press.

For more information, including how to join, please visit

www.sfs.org.uk